The Role of
the Church in Aging

Implications for Policy and Action

The Role of
the Church in Aging
Implications for Policy
and Action

Michael C. Hendrickson, M. Div., M.Th., Ph.D.
Editor

The Haworth Press
New York • London

The Role of the Church in Aging: Implications for Policy and Action has also been published as *Journal of Religion & Aging,* Volume 2, Numbers 1/2, Fall 1985/Winter 1985-86.

The Haworth Press, Inc., 28 East 22 Street, New York, NY 10010-6194
EUROSPAN/Haworth, 3 Henrietta Street, London WC2E 8LU England

Library of Congress Cataloging in Publication Data
Main entry under title:

The Role of the church in aging.

   "Has also been published as Journal of religion & aging, volume 2, numbers 1/2, Fall 1985/Winter 1985-86"—T.p. verso.
   Proceedings of the National Symposium on the Church and Aging, held in Zion, Ill., Sept. 1984 and sponsored by the Luthern Council in the USA.
   Includes bibliographies and index.
   1. Church work with the aged—Congresses. 2. Aged—Congresses. I. Hendrickson, Michael C. II. National Symposium on the Church and Aging (1984 : Zion, Ill.) III. Lutheran Council in the USA.
BV4435.R65   1986   261.8'3426   85-17564
ISBN 0-86656-482-9
ISBN 0-86656-483-7 (pbk.)

The Role of the Church in Aging

Journal of Religion & Aging
Volume 2, Numbers 1/2

CONTENTS

The Role of
the Church in Aging

Implications for Policy and Action

Preface:
The Church and Aging

The purpose of the *National Symposium on The Church and Aging* held in Zion, Illinois, September 1984, was to review the current status of the religious sector's involvement in the field of aging and to identify a series of strategic responses for future policy and action. Over 90 papers were prepared and presented. Seven task forces met to create recommendations for policy, program development and research. This combined issue of the *Journal of Religion & Aging* Volume 2, Numbers 1 and 2 contains selected papers from these proceedings. Volume 2, Number 3 and 4 of the *Journal* will also contain papers from the Symposium. Other records of this event include two 30 minute video tapes and six audio tapes entitled *Images/Issues on The Church and Aging,* which are being released by Augsburg Publishing House, Inc., Minneapolis, MN.

The National Symposium was the culmination of a four year effort. Initial stimulus came from a growing recognition of the need to increase the religious sector's involvement in aging and long term care in substantive ways in order to meet future challenges. Support and encouragement came from a host of professional scientists in the field of aging, public policy makers, researchers, educators, and long term care providers as well as from church body leaders both lay and clergy. Individuals such as Dr. James Birren, Executive Director of the Andrus Gerontology Center, University of Southern California, Dr. Robert Butler, Former Director of the National Institute of Aging, Congressman Claude Pepper, Chair of the House Subcommittee on Long Term Care, Dr. Sylvia Sherwood, Director of the Social Gerontological Research Department, Hebrew Rehabilitation Center for the Aged, and Olaf Kassa, Former President of The American Association of Retired Persons were early supporters as well as key representatives from each of the sponsoring church bodies.

The Symposium has been referred to by some as a *"White House*

Conference on Aging for the Religious Sector. '' Indeed, the comparison is somewhat appropriate. It was decidedly a working conference with a demanding schedule encompassing both formal presentations and task force meetings for the stated purpose of creating major recommendations for deliberation and action by the religious sector.

Briefly, the Symposium sought to:

1. Examine issues in aging, with an emphasis on implications for religious sector response;
2. Document and evaluate the church's past and present involvement in establishing directions for national policy and program development in the field of aging;
3. Discuss values and aging, and derive theological implications for use in shaping the church's own policies and programs;
4. Strengthen the religious sector's involvement in national aging research and identify a research agenda on religion and aging;
5. Define the church's role in the field of aging and develop strategic recommendations for ministry to and with the aging.

Symposium topics covered a broad range of issues from the role of the church as a generator of social and personal meaning, an enabler, advocate, and educator of older persons, to how the church's facilities and resources might be better structured to serve as a primary provider of housing and formal services. Questions were also raised as to how collaborative research efforts between scientists and religious leaders interested in aging might be promoted.

While the Symposium was sponsored by the Lutheran Council in the USA, it was designed to reflect the religious and social pluralism of the nation. Representatives from a wide spectrum of the nation's religious community were involved and contributed to the proceedings. Among the 110 participants selected were older adults, parish pastors, directors of social service agencies, retirement housing and long term care institutions, district and national church executives and staff, seminary and college faculty, together with experts from government, health, welfare, education, and gerontology.

The articles contained in this issue explore the multidimensional nature of aging as well as key issues related to meeting the needs of an expanding elderly population. Subsequent issues of the *Journal* will also include articles on the church's current aging programs as well as special topics in aging.

Michael C. Hendrickson, M. Div., M.Th., Ph.D.
Guest Editor
Project Director & Chair
National Symposium on the Church & Aging

The Role of the Church in Aging: Implications for Policy and Action

Michael C. Hendrickson, M.Div., M.Th., Ph.D.

ABSTRACT. The rapidly aging population in America presents a major challenge to societal institutions. Health and human service systems are attempting to respond to the complex and multidimensional problems of the older population. Yet, due to the unique issues which the elderly face and the limitations of health and human service providers to respond to this population, additional societal responses are required. The religious sector is called to assume various roles, functions, and responsibilities in meeting the needs of the elderly population. In order to fulfill this task, the church must: (1) create an informed leadership; and (2) establish a nationally coordinated coalition dedicated to aging which has wide institutional support from the various church bodies.

Of all the difficult issues facing this nation, perhaps, none is more urgent or complex than responding to the changes being wrought by a rapidly aging population. Predominate of these are new requirements for human services and the need to develop appropriate vehicles to more fully and effectively tap the incredibly rich reservoir of human resources which the elderly represent. Aging also represents one of the most revolutionary developments in recent human history; a direct by-product of a medically and technologically advanced society. Solutions to old problems have created new ones which will challenge our collective imagination and resolve. No other civilization has had as large a number of its population living to extreme old age. Images of life and death, presumptions of what constitutes the stages of life's experiences as well as how to establish social worth or measure productivity, are being severely challenged by findings from gerontological studies and the existence of elderly

Michael C. Hendrickson is Senior Research Scientist, Center for Health and Social Services Research, Associate Professor, Health Services Administration, University of Southern California, President, Retirement Systems Corp. of America Los Angeles, California 90089.

persons themselves. The church, like all other major social institutions, must seek to understand the implications which this massive
tidal wave is having on its structure and programs. Perhaps, the
greatest danger is one of under response to this demographic imperative by failing to retool and reorient ourselves and our social institutions.

THE DEMOGRAPHIC IMPERATIVE

Fortunately, many public leaders, especially health and social
service professionals, are aware that both the number and percentage of persons 65 years of age and older has risen dramatically.
Since 1900, the age structure of American society has experienced
the baby boom of post-World War II, a rapid decline in the birth rate
between 1960 and 1980, and a profound rate of growth in the size
and proportion of those over 65. To measure the magnitude, consider the following. In 1900 four percent of the population was over
65. Today, there are over 23 million which represents over 12 percent of the population. In 15 short years, this cohort alone will increase to about 34 million (Taeuber, 1983).

However, in order to grasp more fully the rapidity of changes oc-
curring, consider the number currently between the ages of 55 and
64. They are the immediate "young elderly." According to the national 1980 census, those between 55 and 64 numbered 22 million or
about 9 and 1/2 percent of the population (Taeuber, 1983). In considering the immediate future (1985-2000) we need to reflect on the
level of impact which 48 million retirees and elderly, over 20 percent of our population, are having on our way of life.

These projections are not speculative. Those who will be over 65
during the next 50 years have already been born. Additionally, it
should be noted that those 75 years old and over will more than tri-
ple during this same period of time. Those who are currently 25 and
older will belong to this group. Thus, America is steadily changing
from a youth to an older adult population, a fact which is just beginning to be reflected in our societal orientation. Recent issues of two
popular weekly magazines devoted major portions of their copy to
the implications which this shift in population is having on governmental, health and human services, and economic structures and
practices. It is becoming increasingly clear that no segment of society will be left untouched by the changes which these figures por-

tend. And the church most assuredly is experiencing similar shifts in age distribution among its membership. Indeed, if figures related to the age distribution of church leadership are any indication of parishes as a whole, the average age of those active in the church is almost three times greater than the national average (Jacquet, 1983). Thus, the future of the nation as a whole and the church in particular will be most dramatically shaped and marked by the elderly.

TO WHOM DO THE CONCERNS
OF THE ELDERLY BELONG?

A concomitant result of an aging society is its greater demand for health and human services. This demand is growing at such an alarming rate that it is placing unmanageable pressures on all sectors of the health and social service systems. Today those over 65 utilize health services at a rate far greater than all other adults. Studies conducted during the 1970's reveal that while the elderly comprise only 11 percent of the population, their combined costs represent about 29 percent of the nation's total expenditure for health care. In real dollars, this amounted to $2,026 per person or about three times the amount spent by those under 65 (Gibson & Fisher, 1979). Further, federal medicare costs indicate that costs for health care for older persons have tripled between 1979 and 1985 with no significant change in current laws or available services (U.S. Congress, Congressional Budget Office, 1985). The intensity of pressure being placed on these systems can only be appropriately understood by recognition that at any one time only 5 percent of the elderly population are residents of long term care institutions. Ninety-five percent continue to live either in their own homes or within community-based settings. The elderly are literally flooding the health system which is viewed by seniors and general public alike as the principal or primary service system for the elderly. For example, they enter hospitals twice as often and stay twice as long as well as visit physicians 25 percent more often than all others (Kovar, 1983).

HEALTH CARE AND THE ELDERLY

While rate of service use is one issue, appropriateness of care is another. Recent research reports indicate that the services most elderly persons receive are not necessarily appropriate to their needs. The elderly present problems which the current health and human service system did not anticipate and is not in large measure organized to address (Hendrickson & Gustafson, 1979). As a consequence, they utilize services which are most easily available or compensated even though many of these may be inappropriate and most of their real needs often go unattended. The elderly tend to suffer from a wide array of social, psychological, and economic impairments which share a symbiotic relationship with their physical illnesses. They have more pain and discomfort, experience greater limitations with daily living, spend more days in bed and suffer more often from depression than other adults. Their needs are multidimensional, chronic in nature and require the kind of therapeutic and personal care services which have not been traditionally offered by health and human service organizations or on a long term basis (Federal Council on the Aging, 1981).

Currently, the health system is locked into an orientation which is focused on the curing of acute infections and diseases. Physicians, who are primarily trained to deal with acute illnesses, have their practices organized by either organ or disease groupings. The key approach of the majority of medical practice entails the use of diagnoses as the means by which health problems are framed and treatment plans established. Institutional facilities, hospitals, clinics, as well as most nursing homes are also organized and structured to treat patients on the basis of diagnoses. However, as previously mentioned, the elderly, especially those who are most frail, have multiple diagnoses and suffer from problems which effect their health status but are generally not addressed by most health professionals (Hendrickson & Gustafson, 1979). Yet, the problem is not a matter of sincerity or provider intentions. One cannot fault those within the health system alone for the problem. Rather, there is a significant discrepancy between what services the system has readily available or for which compensation is given and the real needs of the elderly.

In response to the types of problems which the elderly present, diagnosis is rendered essentially inadequate. Instead of diagnoses, entire new approaches which incorporate multi-functional assessments of health status indices are being successfully utilized with the elderly. These approaches are predicated on the symbiotic nature of the ailments which are normative among elderly persons. Rather than the "rule out" strategy of diagnoses, these approaches consider how a variety of factors will work together to create physical and functional problems. Unfortunately, these approaches have not yet been widely adopted. Currently, only a few health professionals make use of them and hardly any of these are physicians.

Besides not receiving appropriate care for many of their needs, the elderly often suffer additional impairments as a result of their encounters with the medical sector of the health system. A recent Institute of Medicine report on Aging and Medical Education (Dans, 1978) provides ample illustrations as to how current medical practices and procedures can present a real threat of iatrogenic illness to older adults. The report noted that the elderly are often subject to surgical procedures and drugs which can produce side effects that result in further disabilities. Other studies have substantiated that as many as 30 to 40 percent of those currently being placed into institutions such as nursing homes belong in less restrictive, more family type environments (Hendrickson & Gustafson, 1979; Kane et al., 1980).

Clearly, alternative service arrangements must be found for even the frail elderly for whom the greatest amount of the health care dollar is expended. Once elderly persons are moved unnecessarily from their homes and neighborhoods where they want to stay, to institutions where they do not want to go, their health status decreases dramatically and they quickly become dependent upon institutional services. Family resources are depleted by the Medicaid program's "spend down" provisions to the point where there may no longer be a home left to go to even if they could be discharged from a nursing home. Most gerontologists, health planners, and public analysts agree that the elderly must have support systems which are not biased in favor of the medical/institutional model, even though some of such services might be needed along the way. Ultimately, the goal should be to develop programs which will coordinate personal care and housing arrangements which will insure independence and self care life styles for as long as possible.

Perhaps, the most significant problem among the elderly, one which tends to affect both the relatively well elderly as well as the frail old, is that of depression. Those over the age of 65 account for nearly 25 percent of all suicides committed in this country although they represent only 11 percent of the population (Taueber, 1983). As one senior scholar has personally testified, "aging is not something for sissy's because it often brings experiences of real pathos"

(Sittler, 1984). Depression results most often from a profound loss of personal and social meaning. With the elderly especially, old centers of meaning are displaced by the dying of friends, relatives, spouse, in addition to a marked increase of disabilities which interfere with active daily living. Nearly 45 percent of those living in their homes or in community settings suffer quietly from some major impairment. This represents about 11 million persons. Women are particularly vulnerable since over 60 percent of those over 65, live alone or with relatives other than their spouse (Taueber, 1983). These are also the persons who are most dependent upon an informal support system for assistance with active daily living requirements. Thus, if anything were to happen to their informal care giver, they would likely become candidates for institutionalization.

In summary, America's elderly are both increasing rapidly in numbers and find themselves in the difficult position of suffering from functional impairments, with fluctuating levels of disability, and thus dependent for services on a health and human service system which cannot adequately meet their needs. The size of this dependency can only be realized by examining the costs for personal health care among the elderly. Of the total $219 billion spent in 1980 for personal health care, $64.5 billion or 29 percent was spent by seniors. This amount will likely rise to $167.5 billion (this represents a 160 percent increase) during the next 55 years. By contrast, for those under 65, expenditures are projected to increase only 30 percent (Rice & Feldman, 1983). Clearly, in times of austerity, governmentally supported services for the elderly, who are oftentimes also the poor and disabled, will be severely reduced.

Finally, alternative arrangements must be found to meet the future needs of the elderly; arrangements which promote quality of life, continued independence and yet are affordable and cost efficient. To date, the vast majority of attention and effort has focused on 5 percent of the population which is institutionalized. What is required is a greater concern for both the frail elderly who continue to live within community settings as well as the well elderly whose lives may become impaired due to lack of continuous involvement in meaningful activities such as becoming providers of needed services for other older adults. Quite simply, the health and human service system cannot provide the majority of services which older persons will require in larger quantities. This is obvious from a cost as well as appropriateness of care perspective. Others within society must be willing to respond.

THE CHURCH'S ROLE IN AGING:
STRATEGIC RESPONSES TO NEW CHALLENGES

While the church has been an active participant in the field of aging, especially in performing roles of support for social engagement, the needs of today's elderly require new responses. The question is, what should the church's role be in aging? Given a pluralistic social context, what are the various roles, responsibilities, and functions which the religious sector should assume as compared to those appropriately belonging to health, social services, the government, the welfare system and education? How is the church's involvement in aging currently perceived? Is that perception appropriate, given the church's collective resources and capacities? As previously mentioned, the changes being wrought by this nation's demography represent an imperative which can only be ignored at great peril. This changing aging structure is having profound consequences on the nation's entire economic, political, social, health and human services systems into the next century. Aging is not just a social issue but a major force for change.

Historically, churches, synagogues, and other religious organizations have long played a vital role in the lives of older Americans. For example, they have been the unquestioned generator of personal and social meaning for hundreds and thousands of Americans, especially those who currently constitute the elderly population. Indeed, the current elderly are the ones who financed and built the majority of the parishes, church-related schools, as well as the social service and health facilities affiliated with religious organizations. They also made the churches into one of the largest network of voluntary associations in America. A recently completed survey on American values indicated religion has penetrated virtually every dimension of American experience and is a stronger determinant of values than any other single factor. Thus, the significance of the religious sector's organizations in the lives of people, especially the current elderly, is undisputed (Pollack, 1981).

If the health and human service systems are not appropriate and/or able to serve as the primary systems of response for the vulnerable and frail elderly, to what extent can the church assume this role? There are those who would suggest that the church is having difficulty assuming the role of a "gap-filler" and that it does not have the organizational or human resources to extend itself beyond its current level of effort. The appropriateness of the religious sector serving as a principal provider of services for the elderly can be supported for a number of reasons. First, it represents a multi-institutional multi-dimensional, strategically dispersed set of facilities and agencies which are in close proximity to where the majority of older persons live. There are currently more than 500,000 local churches and synagogues in the United States with a reported membership in excess of 140 million whose capital assets have been estimated to exceed $150 billion (Brotman, 1981). Second, churches, collectively, have been the main gatekeepers of the volunteer resources in this country. As such, they are strategically poised to organize and equip the volunteers needed to serve as informal care givers for the frail elderly.

A recent report to the United States House of Representatives Select Committee on Aging (1980) identified the church as a preeminent representative of the voluntary sector which should be encouraged and enabled by the federal government to assume a more primary role with respect to the elderly (Select Committee on Aging Report, 1980). Also, a recent Gallup poll on American volunteerism indicated that nearly 16 million Americans volunteered 1.6 billion hours for a dollar value of 13.7 billion through religious organizations alone, which is more than twice the number given through any other charitable organization (Jacquet, 1983). This, of course, is in addition to actual dollars raised for operating expenses. Given the magnitude of the resources available to the religious sector, it is difficult to accept the notion that the church does not have the means to provide greater services to an aging population.

A third reason why the church represents a viable alternative support system for the elderly lies in the type of resources available and appropriateness of its purpose and mission to the needs of older persons. Use of a formal/informal family surrogate model; the offering of multiple educational, counseling, and social support programs; and the utilization of a mixture of volunteers from all ages, including the current elderly, as well as professional staff, are organizational advantages of the church which are noted as distinct and essential (U.S. Congress, House Select Committee on Aging, 1980). It is also more likely that the church would seek out creative alternatives for keeping the elderly in their homes or communities and out of institutions longer than either the health or social service systems would or could achieve. Churches have a vested interest in maintaining the elderly as vibrant members of their parishes and neighborhoods.

While the religious sector has many organizational and programmatic advantages which would enable it to serve as a primary provider of a wide spectrum of services for older adults, there are several issues which must be addressed and resolved before these can be fully utilized and directed to meet these new challenges. Current programs for the elderly within the church run a gamut from traditional religious programs such as Bible studies for seniors and transportation for worship to special social clubs and programs, and the sponsoring of new social support programs such as adult day care centers, retirement housing, or homemaker services. The services most commonly offered by churches, then, are those which focus on social opportunities, transportation for religious events, fellowship, in-home visitation and spiritual counseling. When individuals require heavier or more personal care, the church has generally assumed that the formal health and social system should and could handle these.

There can no longer be an assumption of reliance that public subsidized programs will provide the basic necessities and leave the private volunteer sector free to concentrate their activities on life enriching activities. With the rapid increase in the number of extreme old living in community settings, there is an urgent need to create a broader base of support services that assist people with the essentials of living. Nearly, 80 percent of those over 65 in this country who are still living within community settings, suffer from at least one chronic condition, and multiple conditions are commonplace for the elderly (Rice & Feldman, 1983). This represents a new challenge for local churches and synagogues to address. Unfortunately, to date, few have exerted any systematic effort to identify support needs of older adults within their immediate communities.

Two extremely important tasks are required to enhance the church's capacity to become a primary provider of services to community based elderly and an influential force in the lives of older Americans. Clearly, there must be a concerted effort to develop a more informed and better equipped leadership. There must be a systematic exploration of the major issues and problems facing the elderly today and for the near future. Finally, there must be an enabling and support system which will serve to stimulate and link local, regional and national activities together in a rational and coordinated manner. Without a knowledgeable and committed leadership or the advantages of a nationally coordinated coalition of religious organizations dedicated to aging and the elderly which has wide institutional support among the various church bodies, the danger of under responding to the demographic imperative will persist. And the churches' own future as a viable component of society will be severely threatened.

The National Symposium on the Church and Aging, held in September 1984, and attended by over 120 leaders from the religious sector represents one effort to develop a more informed and committed leadership. Another effort currently under way is the development of a thirty-three unit Concentration on Aging within the seminary curriculum at Luther/Northwestern Theological Seminary in St. Paul, Minnesota. Similar efforts to these are required if this need is to be adequately met.

Certainly, there are several methods by which the religious sector can increase its involvement, and thereby its influence, in the field of aging aside from developing more innovative and meaningful programs to meet the needs of community based vulnerable and frail elderly. Leaders of the religious community need to become more active participants in shaping national policy with respect to aging. But, in order to participate in these discussions, representatives of the religious community must translate their concerns within the context in which public policy is developed. This includes both advocacy for or against specific pieces of legislation which affect the lives of the elderly, a role which several within the church are already quite familiar.

However, one important additional arena to consider is where policy research priorities are determined. Especially with respect to deriving innovative alternatives to existing programs, policy research priorities for such agencies as: Health Care Financing Administration (which is responsible for the Medicare program) and the Administration on Aging (which handles many of the social service or community based programs for the elderly) should be of interest to leaders from the religious sector. Also, the research priorities established for the National Institute of Aging (which is responsible for much of the basic research currently being conducted on the aging process or treatment modalities) should also reflect the interests of the religious community.

However, to achieve this level of influence, the church needs to become an active participant in contributing to knowledge about aging and the elderly. Because living to an extreme old age is a recent phenomenon there are few clues from the past on how to best manage this development. And science, which helped to create this new possibility, is not able to provide answers to the question of how to increase the value of life to correspond to this new extension of time. Because aging is a social as well as personal phenomenon, nearly 48 million persons in the next twenty years will experience it together. Efforts to create a more informed public about the dimensions of aging will be a major task itself. The church should become a repository of current information on aging, the increasing needs of the elderly and alternative services available. This educational and facilitative function is something which all churches could easily begin to do without a great deal of additional assistance or orientation.

Ultimately, the religious sector needs to become more vested in the issues of aging because these will undoubtedly lead towards greater explorations of the interior (albeit, spiritual) fabric of the human experience. Within gerontology, lies the possibilities to exchange metaphors between various disciplines about human existence including insights gained from a religious, scientific or social perspective. Hopefully, these exchanges will result in an upgrading of the metaphors associated with aging to benefit persons of all ages but especially our seniors. Ultimately, the church's need to become more fully invested in the field of aging should not be driven simply out of sympathy for the plight of the current old, but rather out of a concern for justice and from the perspective of enlightened self interest. For the elderly that we seek to understand and serve ultimately include ourselves.

REFERENCES

Brotman, H., & Brotman, C. (1981) *Chartbook on aging in America.* Washington, D.C.: U.S. Government Printing Office.

Dans, P. (1978). *Aging and medical education.* Washington, D.C.: Institute of Medicine, National Academy of Sciences.

Federal Council on the Aging. (1981). *The need for long term care: Information and issues.* (DHHS Publ. No. 81-20704). Washington, D.C.: U.S. Government Printing Office.

Fischer, C.R. (1980). Differences by age groups in health care spending. *Health Care Financing Review,* 1(4): 65-90 [HHS Publ. No. 03045, Washington, D.C.].

Hendrickson, M. (1985). *The role of the church in aging: Implications for policy and action.* New York: Lutheran Council in the USA.

Hendrickson, M. & Gustafson, J. (1979). *An integrated approach to review: A demonstration and evaluation of a long term care program.* Minneapolis, MN: Foundation for Health Care Evaluation.

Jacquet, C. (ed.). (1983) *Yearbook of American and Canadian churches, 1983.* Nashville: Abingdon Press.

Kane, R.L., Solomon, D.H., Beck, J.C., Keeler, E., & Kane, R.A. (1980). *Geriatrics in the*

United States: Manpower projections and training consideration. Santa Monica, CA: Rand Corporation.

Kovar, M.G. (1983). *Expenditures for the medical care of elderly people living in the community throughout 1980. National medical care utilization and expenditure survey, Data report No. 4.* (DHHS Publ. No. [PHS] 84-20000). Washington, D.C.: National Center for Health Statistics, Public Health Service.

Pollack, W. (1981). *American values of the 1980's.* Connecticut Mutual Life Insurance Company Special Report.

Rice, D., & Feldman, J. (1983). Living longer in the United States: Demographic changes and health needs of the elderly. *Milbank Fund Quarterly/Health and Society.* 61(3).

Sittler, J. *Exploring the multiple dimensions of aging.* Paper presented at the National Symposium of The Role of the Church and Aging, Zion, Illinois, September, 1984.

Taeuber, C. (1983). America in transition: An aging society. *Current Population Reports* (Series P-23, No. 128). Washington, D.C.: U.S. Bureau of the Census.

U.S. Congress. Congressional Budget Office. (1985). *Long term care: Actuarial cost estimates.* Washington, D.C.: U.S. Government Printing Office.

U.S. Congress. House Select Committee on Aging. (1980). *Future directions for aging policy: A human service model.* 96th Congress. Washington, D.C.: U.S. Government Printing Office.

Exchanging Metaphors
Between Science and Religion:
Constructs Which Shape
the Church's Response

Martin J. Heinecken, B.A., B.D., M.A., Ph.D.

ABSTRACT. Since the meaning of a word is its use in a sentence and every discipline develops its own specific language, the terms "science" and "religion" are defined in order to circumscribe the legitimate fields, to determine the limitations of each, and finally to suggest their interrelations. This involves the distinctive metaphors employed in each area. In order to apply this to the problem of ethical decision-making related to aging issues, the field is further limited on the side of "religion" to the "Christian" religion and, even more narrowly, as this is witnessed to by one standing in the Lutheran tradition. A "contextual ethic" is set forth in the context of six basic affirmations: (1) the unconditional love of God to all His creatures; (2) the sinfulness of all human beings; (3) the justification of sinners by faith alone without the works of the law; (4) the necessary distinction and interrelation between "justice" and "love"; (5) the civil righteousness "of which all human beings are capable"; and (6) the individual's "standing place" in life.

Ethical decisions are made by the Christian within this inclusive context, including also the whole sphere of contemporary "secular-scientific" knowledge. Matters of public policy, which involve ethical decisions, however, cannot be dictated by any "sectarian" religious views in a pluralistic society, but only on the basis of reason and what is in accord with commonly accepted moral standards and for the common good. Arriving at such decisions requires the working together of all concerned, specifically "science" and "religion."

Martin J. Heinecken is Professor Emeritus, Lutheran Theological Seminary, Philadelphia, Pennsylvania.

17

I. "SCIENCE" AND "RELIGION"

In *any* human relations, the use of words and metaphors is crucial. We function as human beings only because we can address one another with understood signs, verbal or otherwise, and so elicit a free response from an equally centered self. This involves the I-Thou relation which fully respects the integrity of the other person and never pushes him or her around, as in I-It relations. This I-It relation, however, also has its legitimate place and has brought us to the space and computer age.

Yet there is the tyranny of words with which we continue to confuse and abuse each other. The philosopher Wittgenstein (1958) has said that the meaning of a word is its use in a sentence. There is not a word in any language that was not conceived by someone to serve a specific purpose. New words and new languages are being created all the time. Thus, each science from physics to gerontology has its own jargon as does theology, and if we are to deal with the concerns we share as human beings, we will have to find a common language.

Wittgenstein (1958) also said that a sentence is always in a context, a context which will have to be taken into account. For this he used the much abused expression "language games." There are all kinds of games: card games; board games; games of skill or brawn or intellect; games of competition only with oneself, or with other human beings, or with forces of nature. They all have certain similarities and differences, each with their own rules to be followed. No one faults the chess champion for not twinking the "tiddle-de-wink" into the "thing-a-ma-jig," or the homerun king for not making a touchdown.

So it is with the language of every discipline with its own understood jargon and its own rules meant to achieve a certain purpose. No one need fault one language for not doing what it does not intend to do. The communication of information is not the only function of language. The cheers at a football game are intended only to pump up the adrenaline. There is the language of love, or of abuse, or of ridiculing: the surgeon calling for his instruments at an operation which means life or death; a mother cooing to the babe at her breast; an aroused prophet reading the riot act to a smug and self-righteous people; a priest presiding at a celebration of holy communion.

Humpty Dumpty told Alice, "When I use a word it means exactly what I want it to mean. The only question is, who is to be master. The adjectives I can handle, it is the proud verbs with their nasty tempers that give me trouble" (Carroll, 1946, p. 223). It is the *verbs* in the language of the Hebrew-Christian scriptures that are hard to handle with their pride and their tempers, ranging from fearful condemnation to unconditional acceptance in love.

II. THE CHRISTIAN "RELIGION"

If then there is to be meaningful dialogue between science and religion, terms should be defined. Religion may not be at all good, and considering all the superstitions connected with religion, it is the scientist's task to debunk those superstitions. And it may also be that Jesus, the Christ, is not the founder of another of the world's religions, but that he came to put an end to all false religions, including that of Christianity.

It all depends on what is meant by "religion." This word has two possible derivations. It may be derived from "religare," which means to bind together again, the same root as for "ligament." So religion "religaments" that which belongs together but has become separated, and to the extent that it does that, religion is good and is the Christian affirmation that in Jesus, the Christ, God himself unites alienated human beings with the source of their being. He reunites fragmented human beings into integrated ones. He reunites them with each other without which they cannot be whole, and he will bring the whole creation to its intended fulfillment.

The second derivation is from the word "relegere," meaning to *retell*. There is no religion which does not retell the reputed acts of its gods or god. This would rule out regarding as religious the avowed atheist who clings to so-called "spiritual values" but has no use for gods, forever interfering in the course of human events to help those who whimper to him or clobber those who thumb their noses at him. There is more kinship between the Hebrew-Christian God who is not a static ideal up in the sky, but who is most intimately involved with the affairs of the world. As well, there is more kinship between this living, active god and the so-called pagan, unpredictable gods than with the philosophers sitting and thinking and spinning *all* the answers to life's problems like the spider out of their own brains, or with the scientists busily flitting like the bee from flower fact to flower fact. Ironically, however, most of these philosophers and scientists also made their oblations to the gods, if for no other reason than "just in case."

Thus, the God of the Judeo-Christian tradition is *the God who acts* in history, although always *in a hidden way.* Therefore, neither fairy tales, nor philosophical speculation, nor scientific experimentation is the way to *know* this living God. "Story" is the only medium by which to get to know him in the sense in which the biblical witness uses that word "to know." "Adam knew his wife and she conceived and bore a child" (Genesis 4:1). "You only have I known of all the families of the earth," says the Lord (Amos 3:2).

On the other hand, both philosophical speculation and scientific methodology can indeed do marvelous things. One of the most helpful metaphors in this connection is the metaphor used by Martin Luther when he speaks of the whole creation, all its creatures, all human beings as the "masks" of the hidden god, "in, with, and under which" he gets all his work done, whether he supplies energy through the sun and the riches within the earth and the sea, or puts that energy to use through all the workers of the world. When two people *know* each other, it is he, wearing their masks, who produces the miracle of a new life; he, wearing the masks of the obstetrician and the gynecologist, who watches over that life; he who empowers the gerontologist, to make the life of the aging more tolerable and to prolong the years of their mortality.

But both the philosophers and the scientists who are true to their task will be the first ones to admit, there are some things for which all their fine brains and their marvelous hands are not furnished. They can prolong life to unpredictable limits, and can even resuscitate corpses to continue their mortal pilgrimage a few years longer. But they cannot conquer death itself, and can do absolutely nothing about those who have already gone down the sewer and are only the fertilizer for that fecund future some envision. They cannot forgive sins, and as the sign that the burden has really been lifted, cause paralyzed limbs to move again. They can perform astounding miracles of their own, but they cannot perform those miracles of Jesus that proclaim that with Him the promised and longed for reign of God has already arrived as the earnest and down-payment of that fulfillment toward which all history moves, but which itself lies beyond history in the new Jerusalem that shall come down to earth as a bride adorned for her husband. That last may be a metaphor which confounds the one who has not learned the jargon, but it is no less confounding to the uninitiated when the physicist speaks of the human body as a region of maximum amplitude of superimposed phase waves.

III. A "CONTEXTUAL ETHIC" BASED ON AFFIRMATIONS

Given this background, it may be easier to offer a Christian response to the problem of ethical decision-making, especially as related to aging issues. This author can only speak out of the Lutheran tradition, held there by a combination of freedom and destiny, as others will speak out of their own traditions. In offering a Christian response to ethical decision-making, a "contextual ethic" is utilized, since the term "situational ethics" has been ruined by "tea and sympathy" sentimentalism and used by some of the Watergate conspirators to justify their shenanigans.

It is important to note we are talking about the church which *has already heard*, i.e., *has been apprehended* by the living God's words—and actions. Therefore, that also implies the whole context of the Christian faith, if it is to be truly contextual. From this total context, which is really a seamless garment and not just a patchwork quilt, a "contextual ethic" is set forth in six basic Christian affirmations.

1. Unconditional Love of God. The basic affirmation is that the one whom Christians name as the one God, who alone is to be worshipped is metaphorically referred to as "a fiery, bottomless abyss of love," or in Kierkegaard's—"an inexhaustible fountain of love that never runs dry" (Kierkegaard, 1946, p. 9). As a matter of fact, there is only one place in the Bible where it is said that "God *is* love" (1 John 4:16). Everywhere else we are told only of *how he acts in his love. All* his actions—whether in judgment or in grace are acts of love. This means love in the sense of "agape"—that is, love which is altogether for the sake of the beloved, and not determined by how much or how little the beloved contributes to the selfish desires of the lover. That is why this God is the only one who can really love in this way without diminishing Himself.

Thus, all God's children are equally beloved. All have equal worth, a worth which is not increased by their contribution to the gross national product or lessened by how burdensome they may become to others. Not one is expendable. Not one is to be used. Each one's integrity is to be preserved. And as Kierkegaard said, this applies also to the lilies of the field, "if the lily thought that it was only for its fine raiment that God loved it, would it not, instead of standing dauntless in the field, sporting with the wind, carefree as the gust that blows, not languish and droop, not daring to lift its head'' (Kierkegaard, 1936, p. 23).

Is it necessary to delineate the implications for society's treatment of its elderly, or how the elderly are to think of themselves when they no longer contribute to the gross national product, but continue to have worth in themselves alone? Unless this love of God is acted out for the elderly in a flesh and blood human being who bears the image of that God and reflects it however faultily, the love of God is nothing. The elderly are left alone in their loneliness and despair. There is no one who *"knows"* them.

2. *Sinfulness of Human Beings.* The corollary to the first basic affirmation is that all human beings *are* sinners in a slightly different sense from the one on which Reinhold Niebuhr commented: "When Billy Graham came to New York and called all these boosters for the 'big apple' sinners, *they loved it,"* (Niebuhr, unpublished manuscript). This understands sinners to be in a wrong relationship to their Creator and as a result also to themselves, to their fellow human beings, and to the created world. Likewise, in their limited freedom, humans either exceed their limitations in false pride or do not come up to their possibilities in sloth. Much more elucidation is necessary if this philosophy is not to be dismissed as either unrealistic or hopelessly pessimistic. At least one thing is clear, however. It is once again the great leveler because it is to be distinguished from the fact that no one is perfect. If one is talking about degrees of the always elusive perfection then, indeed, one person may be preferred before another—Walter Payton before Jim Brown, the righteous Pharisee before the immoral slob. But it is precisely as *sinners* that all are equally beloved. No one can exalt himself above another or despise himself as no good.

3. *Justification by Faith.* This would indeed be a monstrous view if it were not for a third affirmation, namely that, as equally sinners and equally beloved we are "justified by faith alone without the works of the law" (Romans 3:21). For this reformation affirmation is not at all a doctrine to be believed so that one may get credit for believing it. It is *an empowering action* during which God not only accepts us as we are, but reorients us and makes us into new beings. It is this that frees us from our misdirected efforts always to justify ourselves, and frees us for our life in the world.

If we *are* sinners and continue to be sinners life-long—even into old age—then this renewal must be a constant recurrence. We must live at all times by the all empowering and all loving work of forgiveness and renewal. Then we can energetically strive toward perfection in our work in the world, where we are to care for the earth and serve the neighbor in *love*.

4. "Justice" and "Love". The fourth affirmation makes a distinction between justice and love without separating the two. The confusion of justice and love takes the cutting edge off each and blunts both into ineffectiveness. Justice is a word with a thousand meanings, but it may perhaps best be taken in the sense in which a little grandson took it when he sobbed his heart out, "It just isn't fair," because the teacher played favorites or changed the rules in the middle of the ballgame. It may also be taken in the sense in which all our news media scream about it—the minorities, the poor through no fault of their own, women, the elderly, the homosexuals, the litigants trying in vain to get a hearing before the court, the prisoners rotting in their hell-holes, children over against parents and vice-versa. Literally *everyone* is in on the act in one way or another: "It isn't fair." Equals should be treated as equals in so far as they are equal, and then differences taken into account. That is why it is so absolutely devastating when people who are only asking for their just rights are made into *objects* of charity by those who are only using them to feather their own nests and make themselves feel "oh so good." If you want it in a metaphor everyone understands, that is when the proverbial "shit hits the fan."

It follows, then, that in a sinful world such as ours the only way to insure justice is not by waiting until people out of sheer good will "do justly and show mercy and walk humbly before God" (Micah 6:8), but by means of just laws, justly enforced without violating the God given rights of any individual. It was only by means of law that the Blacks were given their rights, when the unjust law that forbade them to sit in the front of the bus was changed into a just one that enforced their right to sit where any other human being sits. But in justice this right too is qualified, because there are the handicapped and the elderly, and others who deserve consideration. Moreover, the dialectical relation between justice and love also requires the recognition that a law which has no sanctions, rewarding the obedient and punishing the disobedient, is no law at all. So love must take the form of justice, as Emil Brunner said years ago, "Institutions cannot be loving but only just; on the other hand, you cannot even be just if you are not willing to be loving. You cannot fill the glass completely full unless you are willing to let it run over" (Brunner, 1945). This indicates also that "justice" is other than a strict quid pro quo, tit for tat, but it means meeting the *real* needs of all, however difficult it may be to determine what these are.

Furthermore, only so can the church's advocacy for just laws justly enforced be properly undergirded. It is the height of unrealism to suppose that the giant needs of people all over the world could be met simply by voluntary good will, without just laws.

5. *"Civil Righteousness."* This leads to a fifth affirmation, that, even though all human beings are as sinners under the judgment of his love, this does not mean that they cannot reach magnificent heights of morality. This is stated by St. Paul, "When Gentiles who have not the law do by nature what the law requires . . . they show that what the law requires is written on their hearts" (Romans 2:14-15). So there are *basic* moral recognitions the world around which are equivalent to the moral content of the arbitrarily numbered *ten* commandments (given the time, it could be demonstrated that all the moral relativism in the world notwithstanding—there is enough agreement among the nations of the world including all religions and those who profess no religion to make possible the United Nations Declaration on human rights).

This is what the Roman Church recognizes as "natural law," and Luther recognized as "civil righteousness." It is this common humanist morality, found not only in all the so-called high religions of the world but recognized with devastating clarity sometimes by the greatest scoffers (Voltaire) or by those who in sadness espouse nihilism (Camus). This common morality alone forms a common basis for members of all religions to participate in the public decision-making process which involves ethical questions, not only with respect to the aging, but in all matters involving the well being of human beings and the care of the earth.

So let no Christian presumptuously presume that only a Christian can be moral. If he has any advantage over the rigid moralist, it may be the flexibility to be "lovingly immoral." And by the same token let no Christians presume to think that they have a monopoly on love when the bumper sticker clearly says, "Milk drinkers make better lovers."

6. *"Standing Place in Life."* Finally and perhaps most crucially—considering the way in which it has been abused, there is the factor of what Luther called one's "standing place in life" (Luther, in Tappert, 1959). This has been misunderstood to mean every person's place in a rigidly ordered society with which one is forever stuck. It refers instead to the time and place one occupies in life, by

a combination of destiny and free choice. No one chooses the time and place into which he is born, his parents, his sex, his heredity, his particular gifts or lack of them, or the fact that he is aging. Others are the result of free choice, always within given limitations, without implying that some of them should and could not be overcome. This is so obvious that it seems unnecessary to mention the ethical decision one makes obviously depends upon whether one is a parent or a child, a spouse responsible for a family or "foot-loose and fancy free," or quite helpless and dependent upon others. It makes a difference in which of the legitimate occupations that contribute to human well-being and the caring of the earth one is engaged: whether one is the commander-in-chief of the armed forces or a gardener growing flowers in a monastery garden. Everyone is in multiple relationships, each with their peculiar moral responsibilities and there is no question whatsoever that these will often conflict with each other.

Luther has been accused of making a disastrous distinction between public and private morality. So one of our more stupid and self-righteous members of the White House staff said, "I make no such distinction, I am not a Lutheran." Of course there is a sense in which no such distinction is to be made. If it is wrong to lie to a spouse to hide the fact of unfaithfulness, it is just as wrong for a Congressman to lie to his consitituency in order to hide the fact that he has been embezzling funds. Yet, it should be perfectly obvious that distinctions must be made. A banker may as a private citizen completely cancel the debt owed him personally, but even then he may be constrained conscientiously not to do so because of prior obligations to someone who has a prior claim upon him. But as a banker with responsibilities to his depositors, he has no right to cancel the debt.

IV. ETHICAL DECISION-MAKING

So what does the conscientious person do? He takes all the factors into account: the command of love, the universal moral standards and rights, the positive laws of the land and the international community, the peculiar obligations of his public position as well as his private one. He uses his head and his heart. He searches his conscience, he listens to the wisdom of the ages. He explores the specific tenets of his religion, not only does he seek the advice of pastor or priest or rabbi or guru. He seeks the support of his religious community and other groups of which he is a member, but he also seeks the advice of others who are knowledgable including the doctor, the analyst, the social worker. But whatever decision he makes, he alone bears the responsibility of the decision before God (in the final analysis).

Then, trying in vain to keep his precious escutcheon of self-righteousness clean, he concludes that the decision is the right one and therefore will not let guilt feelings haunt him forever. But decisions are always ambigious and he therefore relies on the all-powerful word of forgiveness, knowing that he is justified by faith alone without the works of the law.

If this scenario suggests a heady position opening fearful possibilities of abuse, *then so be it.* It is part of the freedom for which Christ has set us free. That is why there is sorrow in the heart of God as well as joy over the sinners who repent. As Luther also said, "Our whole life should be one of repentance" (Luther, in *Luther's Works,* 1957, p. 25).

As for public policies where ethical decisions are always involved, it should not be difficult to see the valid analogies. The whole context must be taken into account and all who have something to contribute must have a part in the decision. Then, since we have freedom of religion and a plurality of religions, it should be obvious that the peculiar religious tenets of a group should not be foisted by law upon others—although they may not in justice be forbidden unless they come into conflict with the common good. It is the universally recognized morality that must be upheld, and where there are conflicts, the highest possible degree of justice effecting the highest degree of well-being for all must be the ever elusive goal.

V. CONCLUSION

An extended mixed metaphor may serve as an appropriate conclusion to this discussion. There is the southern folktale about the wooden bowl out of which grandma had to eat her meals, while the rest of the family ate from the good china. When the little girl asked her mother, "Why?" her mother answered, "That's because grandma is old and her hands are shaky." And the little girl said, "Then we'll have to save the wooden bowl for when you are old mother."

A wooden-bowl, a good hearty soup, trembling hands, and a beloved companion to share it. Meals are not meant to be eaten alone. To share a meal with someone means acceptance, openness, the dropping of facades—shades of our carefully orchestrated dinner parties, to say nothing of the cocktail party with its inane chatter of vicious gossip! Meals are for memories; for sharing of the present and plans for the future.

Hence, the most engaging metaphor for the fulfilled creation toward which all history is moving is that of a table fellowship. They shall come from the east and the west and the north and the south and sit down at the marriage supper of the lamb, and the first shall be last, and the last first.

If that is the fulfillment, it is high time that scientists and theologians unite, and share food and drink, memories, present concerns, and hopes for the future. Then, both the riches on the table and the depth of fellowship will be enlarged.

REFERENCES

Brunner, Heinrich Emil. *Justice and the Social Order.* London: Lutterworth Press, 1945.

Carroll, Lewis. *Alice in Wonderland; and Through the Looking Glass.* New York: Grosset & Dunlap, 1946.

Kierkegaard, S.A. *The Works of Love.* Princeton, NJ: Princeton University Press, 1946.

Kierkegaard, S.A. *Philosophical Fragments.* Princeton, NJ: Princeton University Press, 1936.

Luther, Martin. The Large Catechism, In Theodore Tappert (Ed.), *The Book of Concord,* Philadelphia: Fortress Press, 1959.

Luther, Martin. The Ninety-Five Theses. In *Luther's Works: The American Edition,* Volume 31, "Career of the Reformer." Philadelphia: Muhlenberg Press, 1957.

Niebuhr, Reinhold. Unpublished manuscript.

Wittgenstein, Ludwig. *The Blue and the Brown Books.* New York: Harper & Row, 1958.

Aging as a Scientific
and Value-Laden Field of Inquiry

James E. Birren, B.E., M.A., Ph.D.

ABSTRACT. Old age, death, and the nature of aging processes have been subjects of speculation throughout history. People have continuously sought to provide explanations regarding the phenomenon of growing older and the eventuality of death. Early cultural and religious beliefs regarding longevity served to alleviate some of the anxieties about aging. Then, a scientific shift advocated a focus on improving the quality of life, and the development of formal institutions over the years signaled a true belief in the potential for improving conditions of later life. Mobilized research efforts have generated numerous views on aging including the ability of the individual to adapt and the importance of maximizing the functioning of individuals in order to improve life in the later years. An important challenge which may best be broached by religious institutions thus calls upon churches to help individuals set goals which will enhance aging by enabling individuals to find meanings (metaphors) that facilitate the process of adapting to aging.

Important events or phases in the life span are usually surrounded by legend, poetry, rites and mystique. Birth, puberty, marriage, death and other events are culturally embellished with traditions and beliefs. Man's mortality, the fact that we will one day die, is a perpetual puzzle and is emotionally involving. It is not surprising, therefore, that matters of death and old age, and the nature of the processes of aging have been the subjects of speculation throughout history. The mystiques of the past give way slowly to the advances of modern science. Continuing to evolve are ideas we would regard as rational explanations of the natural phenomena of growing older and eventually dying. Wishful thinking lies behind many attempts to free us from the disabilities of old age and to reverse processes of

James E. Birren is Dean, Gerontology, and Professor of Psychology, Ethel Percy Andrus Gerontology Center, University of Southern California, Los Angeles, California 90089-1091.

aging. People have sought through the ages, for example, a magical mud that they might rub on their skin to draw out evil forces that cause aging or to bathe in magical water that would purge the body of all its ills. Wishful thinking becomes incorporated in a culture and its myths about aging (Birren, unpublished manuscript).

BELIEFS REGARDING LONGEVITY

Gruman (1966) identifies three basic themes about human longevity that pervade our cultural background: the Antediluvian theme, the Hyperborean theme and the Fountain theme. The Antedeluvian theme is the Garden of Eden approach that man had the potential for immortality, but through his lack of respect for the deity lost the gift. The struggle for mankind is then to return to immortal life in the next world by self-redemption.

The Hyperborean theme is the view that somewhere in the world there is a group of people who have the secret of immortality or at least very long life. The point in mankind's struggle for immortality is to seek out these remote people who have treasured their near immortality and discover their secret. It is of interest that today there is still a search for the very long-lived people of the world; it is still believed that somewhere in Peru or in India or in a remote part of Russia very long-lived people still exist.

The belief that a remote people have the secret of very long life has been reduced in scale in recent years. Currently, it is thought that such people might live perhaps 20 or more years longer than other peoples. Still, their secret is considered to be worth pursuing. Therefore, there are the treks to out-of-the-way places where fortunate circumstances of living, diet or outlook promote longevity.

The remaining theme is the Fountain of Life theme. This theme suggests that there are healing waters, often in a remote area of the world that must be discovered. These waters purge and heal the body and make one young again. Ponce de Leon sought the Fountain of Youth and our counterpart of the fountain of life theme is found in the popular spas where one "takes the waters." In these spas a mixture of superstition and real benefit will increasingly be separated from the placebo effect (i.e., doing almost anything may bring about a physiological and psychological effect if you believe it will).

The preceeding remarks suggest that there is a rich history of ideas about aging. These ideas, however, are encrusted in myths and superstitions more contrived to deal with mankind's anxieties about his own mortality than with realities. As mankind moves away from magical beliefs about perpetual life he becomes more concerned with the quality of life. Individuals who retreat from simple beliefs in immortal life become more optimistic about the prospects for life extension on this earth. In many ways the history of religious thought is bound up with our aspirations for a long and good life.

EARLY THOUGHTS ABOUT AGING

Early ideas about aging were inextricably linked with religious views of the nature of life which contained the concept of a life after death. Beliefs in immortality of a supernatural nature shifted during the Renaissance. Less and less attention was placed on burying the deceased with goods and tools to serve them in the next world. More thought was devoted to this life and ameliorating its negative conditions, thus augmenting length of life, and beginning to move from ancient religious-cultural views of aging and death to those of science. Modern science, which emerged in the 1800s, clearly has its roots in the Renaissance.

In its complex mixture of superstition, wishful thinking, desire for magic, and elements of theology, religion and philosophy, the culture of contemporary science is hardly totally rational. The motivation underlying modern research on aging is not exclusively based upon a logical, objective and non-emotional basis. Indeed, it has been pointed out that scientific ideas about aging have methaphorical elements in them. This suggests that aging is, in part, an unknown in metaphorical terms. This in and of itself, however, does not preclude progress and one may trade in less useful metaphors for more useful metaphors (Birren and Schroots, 1980). What made the difference between the effectiveness of the scientific period that emerged in the 1800's and what went before was the systematic collection of data about phenomena and the results of experimentation.

One of the main influences of the 19th century scientific period was the collection of demographic data about human beings, their fertility, the frequency of the sexes and their mortality. The French in particular were interested in demography, but their earlier work reporting on differences in mortality rates associated with environment was not encouraged. The idea of empirically investigating differences in the average life associated with different environmental conditions was theologically worrisome. Though earlier suppressed in France, the demographic approach to the study of human existence found its expression in the work of Quetlet (1835). Being a Belgian he could profit by the philosophical ideas of the French Huguenots who escaped into Belgium. His book on the *Nature of Man and his Facilities* (1835) was the initiation of modern research and the systematic study of aging. One of the basic elements of this position is that the conditions of and the influences on human aging are knowable and that this knowledge can be obtained by the systematic pursuit of study or research. This assumption underlies the scientific period: modern science assumes that the basis of human life is ultimately knowable and that knowledge is desirable and useful. There was philosophical resistance to the growth of empirical science in the 19th century. From some theological positions man's quest for knowledge about himself was particularly not appropriate. For example, the religious overtones of resistance to the ideas of Charles Darwin in the last century have still not subsided, although now it is a matter of less an attack on his method of study than of the conclusions he draws from his data.

The 1930s marked the beginning of systematic thoughts about aging and the exchange of information between research projects. In 1933, E.V. Cowdry edited *Arteriosclerosis: A Survey of the Problem* which began to look at the relationships between aging and the changes in blood vessels of which arteriosclerosis is a part. A famous internist at Johns Hopkins University at the turn of the century, William Osler, closely linked aging to the state of the blood vessels in the body and helped to develop a tradition that looked at the consequences of aging as resulting from hardening of the arteries. While the American investigators were stressing the relationship between calcification of arteries and aging of the cardiovascular system, Pavlov and his students in Russia were emphasizing the importance of the central nervous system.

After the publishing of the Cowdry volume on arteriosclerosis the foundation which sponsored it, The Josiah-Macy, Jr. Foundation, realized that aging of arteries did not occur in isolation but involved other aspects of the organism. This lead to a conference sponsored by the National Research Council and the Union of American Biological Societies at Woodshole, Massachusetts on July 25-26, 1937. In 1939, a volume was published that initiated the modern era of gerontology. This was E.V. Cowdry's volume ''Problems of Aging.'' The seminal character of this volume lies in the fact that human aging is regarded as a product of biological, psychological and social forces. Thus began the modern tradition of regarding aging as a multifactorial issue and not caused by a single gene or a single defect in an organ system. The fact that Cowdry's volume was rapidly assimulated is shown by the fact that it was reprinted in 1940 and a second edition was published rapidly in 1942.

On May 23-24, 1941 a major conference on mental health and later maturity was held that was a culmination of much of the thinking of the time. Conferences of that period and the zeitgeist would have culminated in greater impact on social policy, practice and research had not World War II occurred before the proceedings were even published. After World War II, the energies of the country were devoted to housing, educating returning GIs, and getting our institutions back to normal. However, earlier thinking had planted its seeds and there was a momentum set which was to emerge in the later decades.

THE EMERGENCE OF CURRENT VIEWS ON AGING

In 1951 there was a national conference on aging sponsored by the federal security agency, the forerunner of the Department of Health, Education and Welfare. This was followed up by White House Conferences on Aging in 1961, 1971, and 1981. In 1975, the National Institute on Aging of the National Institutes of Health was founded and, in the same period, the Older American's Act established the Administration on Aging within the Department of Health and Human Services. These actions are based on a faith that the scientific method holds a potential for improving the conditions of life in the later years.

A major scientific institution which has had a profound influence on the study of aging in biomedical institutions in America is the National Institutes of Health (NIH). NIH has been effective in promoting basic biomedical research. This research is often carried out within the rubric of a ''war on disease'' by institutes devoted to the study of categorical diseases. These orientations may not be those most suitable to the study of health in relationship to aging, however.

After World War II, categorically oriented disease institutes were promoted. In the spirit of the times, it was thought that the categorical disease institutes would fare better in competition for funds than would the more holistically oriented programs. The National Institutes of Health have been successful beyond anyone's dream in terms of creating a research enterprise, mobilizing congressional support and creating in the public mind the image of waging war on specific diseases. This image is manifested in the public concept of disease as a take-over of the body by a foreign power.

Robert Aldrich, the first director of the National Institute of Child Health and Human Development, once commented that we still suffer from a hangover of this earlier period of the century when our major battles were with infectious diseases. At that time, physicians were taught to seek a single primary diagnosis. It has become apparent that, as infectious diseases were controlled and the population aged, there has been a dramatic increase in chronic diseases and these diseases have become the major killers. Chronic disease is best viewed as not the manifestation of an invasion by a foreign agent but a disorder of the host.

Robertson (cited in Lansing, 1959) once pointed out that "in actuality death is always in some measure accidental." This implies that the last small increment in a stimulus precipitates death in a vulnerable, aged organism. The important point here is the increasing vulnerability of the older organism. Early in the emerging field of gerontology there were many debates about whether there was anything that one might appropriately label "aging." At that time aging was considered to be merely an expression of disease. Today we regard these early debates as beside the point, and consider it more important to specify the energy and the information content of the events that impinge on an organism, as well as its capability to adapt to perturbation. In order to be relevant to aging, the war on disease requires a translation in concept. I believe that increasingly we are going to look at the health of older individuals in terms of environmental interactions and disease-host interactions.

Over the life span there may be a change in the importance of environmental influences, both social and physical. Early in life, there are strong associations between mortality rates and a broad range of factors that can be clustered under the concept of socioeconomic status. Late in life, however, these influences may diminish. For example, the mortality rates of the non-white population, as compared to the white population, are higher in the early years through middle age; however, there is no appreciable difference after age 65. On the one hand, this may be expressing a survival of the biologically fittest in environments which are not necessarily favorable (those who make it to the later years being unusually fit persons). A contrary point of view would hold that, with age, the individual's genetic constitution increasingly expresses itself. More dramatically said, "the genome will out" and, with increasing age, variations in mortality rates may be more controlled by genetic factors. Whether or not there is a decreasing contribution of socio-environmental factors, however, is still debatable. However, what is clear is that we have need for a different orientation to aging than is offered via a categorical-disease approach.

ECOLOGICAL RELATIONS

At the NATO conference on technological developments and aging societies, held at the University of Southern California (Robinson, Livingston, and Birren, 1984), data were reported that indicate that disuse of function can mimic the changes that occur in aging. Shephard (in press) conducted a 10-year longitudinal study of Eskimos who moved into urban areas. Dramatic physiological changes occurred, associated with the fact that the Eskimos' caloric expenditures were reduced by half as a result of their move from characteristic hunting and fishing areas into the city. The Eskimos showed an increase in body fat, lower maximum oxygen capacity, bone demineralization and lower muscle strength.

Many of these characteristics sound like normal aging but, in fact, were in this case associated with altered ecological relationships. It is pertinent to point out that in our current urban environments more and more individuals add "physical loading" to their daily lives, replacing the physical effort lost by sedentary work. That is, we run and engage in other exercise to replace the lost physical effort since we apparently must maintain at least a minimal effort in order to remain in good health. Our concept of added loading can be enlarged to include the use of cognitive functions. Perhaps we will lose our capacity for calculating if we excessively depend on computers; and gone may be the skills manifested by the market clerk who could keep a running tally of a series of individual purchases.

It may also be desirable to speculate about affective loading, although here the principle of loading is less clear. My experiences with the exchange of autobiographies by individuals leads me to suggest that it is a replacement for emotional exchanges that have been minimized by our technological society. I expect that by the year 2000 there will be marked advances in our concepts about aging and, indeed, about how we fit into an evolutionary pattern of aging. Nineteen eighty-three saw the introduction of robots into nursing home care. The friendly little robot machine can do everything we can do—faster, more efficiently. However, the thought of introducing robots into nursing home care brings about some reservations. It is human supporting contact or, if you will, an emotional element that is not met by the machine; and this contact may be essential and life-sustaining in the nursing home context. If culture is the DNA of society, then the *way* we do things is as important to the older individual as *what we do*. Perhaps we are faced with the fact that the decompensating older person is not only in need of energy and information, but also affect. If we wish to maximize function, we must take all three factors into account. Religious communities may be a substitute or replacement for the broken affective bonds resulting from our highly mobile urban societies.

AGING AND WELL-BEING:
METAPHOR, AFFECT AND THE SEARCH FOR MEANING

We all recognize that the use of metaphor has a strong effect on our feelings and motivation. In poetry, the use of metaphor is used to shape our feelings in a powerful way. A salesman may also use metaphor to not only manipulate our feelings, but to shape them toward actions as he desires. In similar ways the use of metaphor by the demagogue may create ways of feeling and mobilize the audience towards the actions desired by the speaker. These thoughts give rise to the question as to the psychological nature and the particular power of metaphor in our current views of aging.

Metaphor is perhaps but a different balance of the three elements that make up all our words. Long ago the Greeks recognized that there were three elements in a word; that is, every word implies knowledge or *cognition* or the process of the mind through which we attach meaning to objects or thoughts or perceptions. Cognition as knowing embraces perception, thinking and remembering. The process of cognition is one of knowing or attaching meaning to events or stimuli (Birren and Hedlund, 1984).

A consequence of knowing or recognizing is the tendency to action; that is, knowing impels us to behavior, either external behavior or new mental effort. Thus, a second element of a word is its tendency to evoke an action. The Greeks use the word *conation* to refer to that conscious tendency to act.

The third element of a word is the feeling it evokes. *Affect* is the complex emotional association evoked by a word. While cognition is the process of knowing or recognizing the information in a word, the affect is the feeling evoked, e.g., love, hate, anger, or anxiety. Words may be chosen to evoke particular feelings.

All of our institutions are, in a sense, metaphors which help us to understand our lives and provide a context for meaning. In turn, the metaphors of life promoted by these institutions affect our current views regarding aging as well as the degree of well-being achieved in old age.

If universities are concerned with the processes of knowing and the market place and politics with the processes of action, there remains a question about which institutions are primarily concerned with the processes of emotion. Here one might suggest that the churches and the entertainment world are the areas in which emotions have their principle expressions. People turn to religious institutions at crucial junctions in their lives when emotions are evoked, such as weddings, births and funerals, and perhaps at the time when children are in transit from childhood to adulthood. Clearly all these institutions have their processes of knowing, action, and emotions yet it is suggested here that they are somewhat specialized in their emphasis on one of the processes and this is not unlike the metaphor itself.

Individuals select to a considerable extent their personal metaphors of their lives and of aging. Bateson (1972) also sees the individual as having the potential for increased self-determination as she/he matures. "Self-determination" in a positive sense is included in the term "wisdom" which Bateson defines as a knowledge of the larger interactive system. This view sees the individual as a part of an overall system. The system is self-correcting because when one part of the system experiences change another aspect of the system must also change or the relationship of the overall system will be jeopardized. A system is defined by Bateson as all one takes in or gives out both conscious or unconscious. Man's advantage over other species is that she/he can alter the environment rather than altering her/himself. Each individual develops a belief system about the world and then confirms his or her belief system by acting as if it were true. Equilibrium is upset if one's beliefs are so out of line with reality (the environment) that environmental changes are not flexible enough to confirm the belief system. The "wise" person is able to understand the environment well enough to know the limits of its plasticity so that she/he does not upset the balance of the system. Thus, how we view the world and the aging process itself affects how we age.

Charlotte Buhler (1968) portrays the ideal individual striving toward fulfillment by living a goal directed life. She defines goals as being active and outgoing and directed toward a positive anticipation and a desire to accomplish. The first goals are determined by biological and psychophysical structures. These "genetic" goals remain as a force throughout the individual's life, but with increasing age these goals can be modified and, for periods of time, replaced by values and beliefs. Buhler postulates four basic tendencies that goals follow: need satisfaction, upholding order or stability, self-limiting adaptation and creative expansion. In Buhler's model, "self-determination" occurs in a life that is directed toward fulfillment of an ultimate purpose.

Self-transcendence or directing one's life toward a purpose greater than oneself is Victor Frankl's (1980) term for the process of self-direction. He believes that one cannot truly fulfill oneself without reaching outside the self and serving others. Maslow (1962) concurs with Frankl in that he sees the self-actualized person as being directed to external causes, but also as being more spontaneous, expressive, less controlled and inhibited and as having higher levels of self-esteem. Rogers (1961) also sees people as striving for self-actualization. He again takes a self-creationist position: "Each person attempts to actualize or develop all of his or her capacities in ways that serve to maintain and enhance life" (p. 7). If these goals are reached, aging will be enhanced as the individual finds the meanings (metaphors) that help him or her adapt to the process of age.

These views of mankinds' quest for meaning in a long life need more attention parallel to our scientific quest for knowledge about aging. Living longer is not just a matter for the laboratory to solve but also is a matter for humanists and humanitarian institutions to aid in the search for meaning in the later years.

REFERENCES

Allport, G. (1955). *Becoming*. New Haven: Yale University Press.
Bateson, G. (1972). *Steps to an ecology of mind*. San Francisco: Chandler Publishing Co.
Birren, J.E. (1984). Health care in the 21st century. In C.M. Gaitz and T. Samorajski (eds.) *Aging 2000: Our Health Care Destiny*. New York: Springer-Verlag.

Birren, J.E. (unpublished manuscript). The history of aging and gerontology.

Birren, J.E. & Hedlund, B. (1982). The metaphors of aging and the self-constructing individual. In, J. Thornton (ed.), *Proceedings, University of British Columbia Conference, 1982.*

Birren, J.E. & Schroots, J.J.F. (1980). Aging, from cell to society: A search for new metaphors. World Health Organization Meeting, Mexico City, 1980, Agenda item 6.

Buhler, C. (1968). *The course of human life.* New York: Springer Publishing Company, Inc.

Cowdry, E.V. (ed.) (1933). *Arteriosclerosis: A survey of the problem.* Baltimore: Williams and Wilkins.

Cowdry, E.V. (ed.) (1939). *Problems of aging.* Baltimore: Williams and Wilkins.

Frankl, V. (1978). *The unheard cry for meaning.* New York: Simon & Shuster.

Gruman, G. (1966). *History of ideas about prolongation of life: The evolution of prolongevity hypotheses to 1800.* Salem, N.H.: Ayer.

Lansing, A.I. (1959). General biology of senescence. In, Birren, J.E. (ed.) *Handbook of aging and the individual.* Chicago: University of Chicago Press. 119-135.

Maslow, A. (1962). *Toward a psychology of being.* Princeton: D. Van Nostrand Company, Inc.

Quetlet (1835). *Nature of man and his faculties.*

Robinson, P., Livingston, J., Birren, J. (eds.) (1984). *Aging and technological advances.* New York: Plenum Press.

Rogers, C. (1961). *On becoming a person.* Boston: Houghton Mifflin.

Shephard, R. (1984). Technological changes the the aging of working capacity. In, Robinson, P., Livingston, J., Birren, J. (eds.) *Aging and technological advances.* New York: Plenum Press.

Knowing Your Age

F. Eugene Yates, M.D.

ABSTRACT. The aging process occurs with overall statistical regularity, consisting of a constant rate of decline in physiological function. While the last century has witnessed an increased average life expectancy, the progress made in extending the lifespan has been deferral of death to a later point in an unchanging maximum life potential of 110 years. Furthermore, even if science succeeds in eliminating diseases which continue to block longer life, with a resultant additional increase of lifespan, the added life would be years of growing old and not of additional good health or youth. Thus, given there is no strong scientific basis for aggressive intervention against the aging process, mankind is called to question the value of spending energy on determining biological age and reflecting upon the apparent worth in focusing on human feelings, attitudes, and values pertaining to issues of life and death, at *all* ages.

It has been said that you are as old as your back. But, from a ''giblets'' perspective one could as well say—as old as your bones, your coronary arteries, your cerebral cortex, your gut, your skin or sexual parts—the choice depending on what's going on at the moment or planned. Imagine a person presenting his 63-year old body to a physician for his annual insurance evaluation. Just as *Consumer Reports* assures us that automobiles typically have 14 systems, each with an independently verifiable repair record, so could the physician go down a check list of the 12 major physiological systems (gastrointestinal, reproductive, musculoskeletal, integumentary, immunological, circulatory—including hematopoietic, respiratory, renal, central nervous, autonomic nervous, endocrine and thermo-

F. Eugene Yates is Director, Crump Institute for Medical Engineering, 6417 Boelter Hall, University of California, Los Angeles, California 90024.

Supported in part by a grant from the Hartford Foundation.

I wish to acknowledge the outstanding contributions of Donald O. Walter and Laurel A. Benton to our studies on aging.

regulatory) and at great expense provide a list of 12 or more "grades." But, did the subject "pass"? Is this system-by-system scoring the way to judge fitness, health, vitality, viability or biological age?

An entirely different basis for judging how old one is could be made on behavioral grounds. As Urquhart and Heilmann have remarked (1984): "Risk-taking and risk avoiding are intrinsic to life itself. Juxtaposing them serves to emphasize the many paradoxes one encounters in threading between risk-taking and risk-avoidance. As we mature, we veer away from the former and toward the latter. The quest for vanished youth during our middle years is often expressed by a shift back toward risk-taking, while extreme risk-aversion is often considered a mark of aging." So what do we say about a 72-year old subject (a real case), recovered from a severe myocardial infarction six years ago and now with heart pains (angina) on exertion and severe occlusive vascular disease proven by coronary artery angiography—who wants a "bypass operation" and permission to ski later this year? Is he a hero, a fool, or an energetic realist? Is he "old" or "young"?

Few feel better about their bodies as time runs on (though fortunately many of us feel better about "ourselves" as we grow older). In the main, we do not like getting physically old. Shakespeare detested old age: "Age, I do abhor thee, youth, I do adore thee!" So did Horace:

> Grey hairs have many evils; without end
> The old man gathers what he dare not spend . . .
> Extols his own young days with peevish praise
> But rates and censures these degenerate days.

And Shakespeare, again, repeatedly in his sonnets saw time as the archenemy:

> Time doth transfix the flourish set on youth,
> And delves the parallels in beauty's brow;
> Feeds on the rarities of nature's truth
> And nothing stands but for his scythe to mow.

To most of our poets aging and senescence are best described as an enlarging catalog of losses. The ultimate loss is of itself; for that we know the statistics and probabilities. For example, Table 1 shows

TABLE 1

(From DeRopp, 1960)

(For 100,000 born alive in the U.S. in 1950)

Age of Cohort (Years)		Number of Deaths	Number of Survivors	Life Expectancy of Survivors (Years)
Past	1	2,722	97,278	69.02
	10	776	96,502	61.48
	20	739	95,763	51.91
	30	1,227	94,536	42.52
Now	- -			
	40	1,920	92,616	33.29
	50	4,506	88,110	24.70
	60	10,004	78,006	17.15
Future	70	18,887	59,189	10.89
	80	28,751	30,438	6.27
	90	24,237	6,201	3.41
	100	6,005	196	1.92
	105	184	12	1.53
	110	11	1	——

the expectation of death and survivability for 100,000 white males and females born alive (for example) on June 1, 1950, in the U.S. It gives information for each decade of life up to the present (the survivors are now nearly 35) and projects into the future based on life expectancies applicable in 1950. (Since then there has been an improvement in the average life expectancy for both men and women in the United States and so the table very likely has some people dying too soon, but not by much.) The pattern in Table 1 is typical for the so-called "developed" countries.

Urquhart and Heilmann (1984) comment very colorfully on such data:

> One can visualize the meaning of these numbers . . . by recalling a cinematic image from many films showing 18th or 19th century battles in which a broad front of foot soldiers marches in attack toward the other side's stationary battle line. As the attacking front marches forward, soldiers are hit by enemy fire, and fall. The advancing line pulls together, side-to-side, and continues. As the soldiers draw nearer to the enemy line, both the density and accuracy of enemy fire increases, and the men fall from the advancing line at an accelerating pace. The ever more depleted line continues to draw together, side-to-side, until finally, as it approaches the enemy

line, the last few men fall, and the battle is over. . . . In the analogy we use here the other side is death, destined never to be overtaken, and the field is marked off not in distance but in years. The field is 110 years "long" . . . Each year's crop of newborns comes up out of their trench, at year 0, and commences marching toward certain death, 110 years hence.

Although in the last century, in developed countries, infant mortality rates have fallen and average life expectancy has increased, the maximum life potential for the human species has remained where it always has been, probably since the origin of our species perhaps 200,000 years ago, and maybe as far back as our separation from the chimpanzee seven million years ago (as estimated by DNA "molecular clocks"). The progress that has been made in extending average lifespan has been *deferral of death to a later point in an unchanging maximum life potential of about 110 years*. Thus, in the U.S. today the average life expectancy for a newborn male is about 70 years and for a newborn female, about 78 years. But these are population statistics. What about your own "personal" age?

It could be that some overall "biological" age of a single person is a descriptor about him at a given moment that is as particular as is his body weight. Certainly, in a room full of 50-year olds, not all will have the same biological age—for example, not all will have the same probability of reaching age 60. Can we tell what those various probabilities are and assign them to individuals? Is there anything physicians can do in an annual physical exam that could assign to a person his own biological age?

CAN BIOLOGICAL AGE BE ASSIGNED?

Of the two strongest determinants of biological age—(1) the particular genes of the person under consideration and (2) his chronological age—we know only the latter exactly. It is likely, however, that we may soon be able to do empirical correlations between genetic measurements on an individual (from white blood cells, for example) and probabilities of his susceptibility to various diseases or of accelerated declines in functions. But today—can we tell about an individual at any age whether or not he is ahead of, on, or behind his "genetically" shaped aging schedule? (He could be accelerating his decline by abusing drugs, or by chronically stressing himself trying to perform in a job that is over his head. Genes say nothing very specific about such matters.) Can we assign a single biological age or is it possible that we have to specify a separate age for each major organ system? Could a person have a 40-year old liver, a 35-year old heart, a 55-year old frontal lobe in his brain, and the skin of an ancient? (Considering the skin—one notices on his own body that the backs of his hands seem more "weathered" than does the skin over his buttocks. Sunlight-induced damage of exposed skin is known to be the basis of that difference. But then, we would have to say that the real "age" of the skin is better given by the unexposed regions.)

In spite of seeming differences, there is an overall statistical regularity in the aging process, consisting of a constant rate of decline in physiological function of most organ systems at about 1 percent of the maximum reserve value at age 30, per year, linearly after age 30. (These declines do not appear to be very sensitive to changes in lifestyle, but cigarette smoking is the great exception. The life-shortening effects of cigarette smoking are so powerful, and so varied, that any analysis of the aging process itself has to be corrected for those effects.)

HOW DOES BIOLOGICAL TIME COMPARE
TO CLOCK TIME?

If we accept the familiar intuitive notion that there is an "external" time that runs smoothly and uniformly (this notion is not physically rigorous) then we can say that "biological time" does not run in a linear, proportional relationship to "external" time. If we define a unit of biological time as an interval over which the probability of dying is at some chosen value, then a unit of clock time (e.g., a day) for an old person would be equivalent to many units of clock time (many days) for a young person. The inverse also holds: a constant unit of clock time dilates as biological time, with aging, i.e., an hour uses up much more of life for an 80-year old than for a 30-year old, on the average. (But oddly, in "psychological" time the reverse is true! The idea that within an individual organism biological time is nonlinearly related to clock time is more poetic than physical, but it does accord with experience and justifies speculation about the nature of biological time. I have commented on that issue elsewhere and will not repeat the arguments here (Yates, in press).)

WHAT IS IT THAT THE MEN OF DEATH USE AS WEAPONS TO BRING US DOWN?

To condense an enormous amount of information, we can say that aging is *not* cancer, it is *not* kidney disease, it is *not* coronary artery atherosclerosis, it is *not* diabetes . . . in fact, it is *not a "disease" at all!* It is an underlying, fundamental, intrinsic process genetically scaled and environmentally conditioned, that progressively increases the likelihood of occurrence of many diseases (including those just mentioned), of accidents and calamities, and of dynamic instabilities resulting in death.

Table 2 shows the gain in expectancy of life at birth and at age 65

TABLE 2

Gain in Expectancy of Life at Birth and at Age 65

Due to Elimination of Various Causes of Death

Cause of Death	Gain in Expectancy of Life (yrs) if Cause was Eliminated	
	At Birth	At Age 65
Major cardiovascular-renal diseases	10.9	10.0
Heart disease	5.9	4.9
Vascular diseases affecting central nervous system	1.3	1.2
Malignant neoplasms	2.3	1.2
Accidents other than by motor vehicles	0.6	0.1
Motor vehicle accidents	0.6	0.1
Influenza and pneumonia	0.5	0.2
Infectious diseases (excluding tuberculosis)	0.2	0.1
Diabetes mellitus	0.2	0.2
Tuberculosis	0.1	0.0

From Life tables published by the National Center of Health Statistics, USPHS and U.S. Bureau of the Census, "Some Demographic Aspects of Aging in the United States," February, 1973.

that would occur if we could eliminate various common causes of death entirely.

It can be seen from this table that with the complete elimination of the top four causes of death of human beings in the U.S. today, the gain in average lifespan would be about 20 years. In other words, by the elimination of major cardiovascular-renal diseases, heart diseases, vascular diseases affecting the central nervous system and all malignant neoplasms, the average lifespan in the United States would be increased from about 70 years today to 90 years, with the maximum life potential remaining unchanged at about 100 years. But, as Cutler (1983) points out:

> The important point must be recognized in this approach of increasing lifespan by eliminating specific diseases that the resultant increase of lifespan would not be 20 years of additional good health or youth but instead 20 additional years of growing deeper into old age. Thus, the elimination of the major diseases of man is not likely to act importantly in uniformly preserving health. The normal aging rate would not be affected and new age-related diseases and dysfunctions would be uncovered. Worst of all, cognitive and related brain functions would all continue to decline at their normal rate in spite of the complete elimination of all these major killers of humans today.

Our various "wars" against heart disease, stroke and cancer are bound to be both increasingly expensive and decreasingly effective. Possibly more valuable would be retarding the underlying aging process itself, from which susceptibility to cardiovascular disease, stroke and many cancers emerges. But we have no idea how to do this.

THEORIES ABOUT THE CAUSES OF AGING

The many different "theories" of aging and senescence scarcely deserve the name; many are tautological or empty formulations, tending merely to restate observations, or else they insist on a partisan, unproved view. We scientists are not ready yet to assert the cause of senescence, but we believe that it belongs to the continuum of growth and development that makes up the normal trajectory of mortal life. Meanwhile, until we understand better, we can merely find palliatives, patches, fixes, and retrofits with technological shopware and glitter. (It would be easy to exhaust the coffers by so doing, as we are already beginning to see.)

For the interested reader I list here some ideas that have been considered as explanations of the aging process. Some imagine that there is a "death gene" that carries an "instruction" that we should age and die. Another view says that aging is "wear-and-tear." Another view says that cells have a genetic limitation on how many times they can divide and after that they become vulnerable to accidents because they cannot reproduce themselves. (But not all our cells normally retain a capacity to divide after we mature. For example, muscle and brain cells don't; those lining the gut do.) In still another view it is assumed that aging is caused by a slow failure of DNA repair mechanisms so that damage to genes by chemicals or cosmic radiation, which is relatively harmless when we are young, becomes increasingly dangerous as time passes because broken genes can no longer be quickly repaired before they fail or act as dysinformation. In yet another view, the byproducts of the normal, metabolic energetics that maintain us are chemicals that can potentially do damage. We therefore have biochemical mechanisms to detoxify these agents, but these mechanisms themselves slowly become overwhelmed with time, possibly by the very toxins they are inactivating. Thus, an autocatalytic process is set up whereby the inactivators become inactivated and subjected to still faster inactivation by toxin accumulation onward into the grave.

As stated (too simply) above every one of these ideas has weaknesses as a theory of aging. However, with some technical fixes and more careful statements of claims many of these ideas are still being developed in the field of gerontology. To acquaint the technically-minded reader with the scientific theories about the aging process I offer the following reading list: DeRopp, R. S. (1960), Curtis, H. J. (1966), Strehler, B. L. (1977), Fries and Crapo (1981), Florini, J. R. (1981), Proceedings of a Conference of the National Institute on Aging (1981), Adelman and Roth (1982), National Institute on Aging Report (1982), Reff, M. E. and Schneider, E. L. (1982), Regelson, W. and Sinex, F. M. (1982), and Cutler, R. (1983).

Among the many ideas in these references, those of Richard Cutler seem to me to make the most sense and deserve special mention. He says that work in his laboratory has been based on three main postulates that make up the working hypothesis to be tested experimentally. These are as follows (in somewhat technical language):

(1) The cause of aging is pleiotropic in nature, being the by-product of normal energy metabolism and developmental processes, (2) The aging process itself is largely one of dysdifferentiation, the slow progression of cells away from their proper state of differentiation, and (3) Longevity of a species is determined by processes acting to stablize the cells' proper state of differentiation against the destabilizing effects of the pleiotropic by-products of energy metabolism and development.

Longevity determinants are postulated to be stabilizers of the proper differentiated states of cells. It is also predicted that the genes responsible for both aging and species' differences in lifespan potentials are the "same" in all mammalian species. Thus, different species age qualitatively similarly because they have the "same" set of genes causing aging and because different lifespan potentials are due to different degrees of expression of the "same" longevity determinants found in all mammalian species.

A fundamental prediction of this working hypothesis is that cells in longer-lived species (such as human) would be found to be inherently more stable in maintaining their differentiated state in the presence of endogenous modifiers such as free radicals because they have higher levels of expression of the same longevity determinants found in all mammalian species.

For further details, consult Cutler (1983).

Any theory about the aging process has to account for the differing maximum lifespans of various mammalian species (e.g., rats live about 4 years maximum, horses 60, humans 110). It must also account for the rather regular, linear decline in physiological organ system functions of a single human individual with time. It ought also to account for those population dynamics of a species or cohort, that was first mathematized by Gompertz to explain population mortality curves. Thus, we ask of these theories that they pertain at the same time to the individual, to a population of such individuals, and to a variety of species! That is a very demanding requirement.

In the absence of adequate theory, we do not know how to assess your biological age, except by empirical studies, and these are not yet definitive. We hope to do better soon. Below is a (somewhat technical) account of our own work on aging, that shows a new approach to determining how old you are.

HOMEODYNAMICS, COOPERATIVITY AND BIOLOGICAL AGE

According to a physical theoria we have developed, called homeodynamics, (extending the earlier concepts of Walter Cannon's homeostasis theory of stability of life, published in 1929) physiological integration (functional coherence) requires cooperativity and modulation (but not necessarily synchronization) among groups of process oscillators. Opposing themes of competition and cooperation, and of activation and inhibition, dominate the dynamics of life at all of its levels. Within an organism the *net result of all oscillatory, interacting processes must be cooperative* to assure stability and persistence. Thus, it is meaningful to seek a measure of cooperativity among processes to assess physiological integration. To do that it is necessary to nominate *a priori* (based on information from past physiological studies), clusters of variables likely to be constrained to dance together in some sense, though not necessarily in close step.

Each of the physiological (homeodynamic) variables contributing to the stability of the system will have some characteristic time interval over which its mean value is established. Its motion around the mean value repeats, so the variance has near-periodic structure (i.e., the motion is periodic or oscillatory). Cooperativity among homeodynamic variables is seen through *"dynamic signatures"* that can be extracted and visualized by plotting the time courses of the clusters of variables against each other, after they are "flashed" in a stroboscopic manner (in a digital computer analysis of the data) to identify any oscillatory properties that may be present.

These are novel techniques that lead to multidimensional plots that can be both personal—that is, descriptive of a particular individual's physiological arrangements—and general, as a measure of the required ("healthy") characteristics of physiological organ systems in human beings. The theory on which all this rests derives from a combination of irreverisible thermodynamics, statistical mechanics and nonlinear mechanics (see Yates, 1982a, b). It will become of importance to clinical medicine only if the "dynamic signatures" can be displayed in a reproducible and comprehensible form, and can be shown to be predictive of future states of health.

DYNAMIC SIGNATURES—CLINICAL VERSION: A MEASURE OF BIOLOGICAL AGE?

We postulated that (among cardiovascular variables) systolic pressure, diastolic pressure, and heart rate would have to cooperate in some manner because they are bound together in performance by various well-known reflexes (such as the barostatic reflexes that keep you from fainting when you stand up suddenly). We applied our new stroboscopic analysis as a sensitive method for exploring rhythmic cooperativity among these variables in normal, ambulatory human beings. Because aging is a process leading to progressive dynamic instability, we expected that it would show up as alterations in dynamic signatures in the circulatory and other systems. We are testing that expectation now. In order to find out the possible mechanisms underlying changes in dynamic signatures, we are also comparing them in normal subjects and in subjects with denervated hearts resulting from heart or heart-lung transplantation.

The dynamic signature approach can also be used to test the strength of coupling between different physiological systems. For example, we can combine the dynamic signatures of cardiovascular variables with those of metabolic, thermal, or respiratory variables (pre-filtered by our stroboscopic methods). When this is done, the intrinsic "choreography" of a dynamic ballet emerges. Its evolution over time should mark the progress of biological aging, according to our homeodynamic theory.

These ideas are new, and just now undergoing clinical testing. They represent a multidimensional, mathematical-physical approach to senescence and aging whose clinical usefulness is yet to be decided.

CONCLUSION

If it is not likely that there will be any major advances in the near future that will extend *youthfulness* into what is now considered to be old age, is it even worth knowing how biologically old one is? Is not it enough just to know whether or not one is satisfied, within reason and within the range of reconciliation and resignation, with his condition, feelings and circumstances at *any* age? Maybe it does not matter whether or not we can measure "health," or "vitality" so as to assign a biological age to an individual. (Perhaps not, but insurance and airline companies care.)

Given that there is not strong scientific basis for aggressive intervention against the aging process, we are left with the now-familiar suggestion that one should choose his parents and grandparents wisely (for their longevity). Preferably, be born female. After that stay away from cigarette smoking. Then, noticing that dietary fat, salt and sugar (statistically) seem detrimental to health beyond a certain minimum intake per day (which I won't go into here), keep the intakes of them low.

Exercise does not have any bearing whatever on cancer, and gives no guarantee that one will not have a heart attack (though it may enhance recovery) but it does make most people feel better and more full of "life"—unless their joints hurt, in which case swimming becomes almost the only tolerable exercise. (Fortunately, it's a good one.) Keeping company with others, including the young and pets, unquestionably enriches and sustains life, regardless of age.

Everything becomes harder to do if health begins to deteriorate badly, but fortunately, in many cases it does not. Consider Edwina MacKenzie who just died on Monday, December 3, 1984. In her 101st (and last) year she hosted 300 acquaintances at a 100th Birthday party, and a year ago on a trip to London was mobbed by fans. (She was thought to be the oldest survivor of the Titanic.) She outlived three husbands. A few days before her death she checked into a hospital not feeling well, and went rapidly downhill and out. This is the classical story of the life and health of a (relatively) disease-free person who does indeed die of "old age." Not many of us will be so lucky because aging increases our susceptibility to a variety of curses which, though not themselves intrinsic to the aging process, all too frequently are invited by it.

Finally, we come to resignation, contemplation, reflection and the assignment of values to oneself, to life; to personal views of man's fate and man's hope. From the beginning of recorded history man has indicated that he knows he cannot look to mere technique to give value to his life—those values arise elsewhere and it is in the formation of one's attitudes about life and death that, now—as then, the greatest power for happiness and health lies.

REFERENCES

Adelman, R. C. and G. S. Roth (1982) *Testing the Theories of Aging.* CRC Press, Inc., Boca Raton, Florida.

Cannon, W. B. (1929) Organization for physiological homeostasis. *Physiol. Rev.* 9: 399-431.

Curtis, H. J. (1966) *Biological Mechanisms of Aging.* Charles C. Thomas, Springfield, Illinois.

Cutler, R. (1983) Species probes, longevity and aging. In: *Intervention in the Aging Process-Part B: Basic Research and Preclinical Screening.* W. Regelson and F. M. Sinex (eds.), Alan R. Liss, Inc., New York, pp. 59-144.

DeRopp, R. S. (1960) *Man Against Aging.* St. Martins Press, New York.

Florini, J. R. (1981) (Ed.) *CRC Handbook of Biochemistry in Aging.* CRC Press, Inc., Boca Raton, Florida.

Fries, J. F. and L. M. Crapo (1981) *Vitality and Aging.* W. H. Freeman, San Francisco.

National Institute on Aging (1982) Report: "A National Plan for Research on Aging," NIH Publication Number 82-2453, September, 1982, Washington, D.C.

National Institutes of Health (1981) "Biological Mechanisms in Aging." Publication Number 81-2194. U.S. Department of Health and Human Services, Public Health Service, Washington, D.C.

Reff, M. E. and E. L. Schneider (1982) "Biological Markers of Aging." NIH Publication Number 82-2221. U.S. Department of Health and Human Services, Public Health Service, Washington, D.C.

Regelson, W. and F. M. Sinex (1982) *Intervention in the Aging Process.* Part B: Basic Research and Preclinical Screening. Volume 3B Modern Aging Research. Alan R. Liss, Inc., New York.

Strehler, B. L. (1977) *Time, Cells and Aging* (second edition), Academic Press.

Urquhart, J. and K. Heilmann (1984) *Risk Watch: The Odds of Life.* Facts on File Publications, New York.

Yates, F. E. (1982a) Systems analysis of hormone action: principles and strategies. In: *Biological Regulation and Development,* Vol. 3A: Hormone Action, R. F. Goldberger and K. R. Yamamoto (eds.), Plenum Press, New York, pp. 25-97.

Yates, F. E. (1982b) Outline of a physical theory of physiological systems. *Canadian J. of Physiol. and Pharmacol.* 60(3): 217-248.

Yates, F. E. Senescence from the aspect of physical stability. University of British Columbia Press (in press).

Informal Care for Vulnerable Elderly: Suggestions for Church Involvement

Sylvia Sherwood, Ph.D.
Ellen Bernstein, M.A.

ABSTRACT. The elderly population in our society has needs which require understanding, advocacy, and service provision. While the formal support system helps in meeting these needs to an extent, it is clearly overburdened and cannot cope with the expanding demand from a continuously growing number of older persons. Thus, the challenge to restructuring society's approach to the delivery of long term care leads one to examine the potential of the informal support system resource pool. While families, as one component of this resource pool, provide a substantial amount of support to their elderly, they themselves need to be supported as well as supplemented. The church can undertake a valuable role by facilitating initiatives to foster and stimulate informal supports and encouraging volunteer support networks.

Once, uncertain sanitation, poor nutrition and infectious diseases like smallpox, typhoid and pneumonia claimed the lives of most people before they reached 65. Today, however, scientific advances and medical breakthroughs have enabled many people to live to age 65 and far beyond. In fact, of all the people who have ever survived on earth to age 65, a majority are alive today and this statistic will continue to be correct to the year 2000.[1]

The over 65 population in America is growing rapidly, and the group over 75 is growing fastest of all. Over the last two decades, the number of Americans over 85 has doubled, and according to Dr. Edward Campion, Chief of the Geriatrics Unit at Massachusetts General Hospital, the tremendous expansion of the elderly population, particularly those over 85, is the single most important epidemiologic trend in health care.[2]

Sylvia Sherwood is Director, Department of Social Gerontological Research and Ellen Bernstein is Director of Technical Publications, Hebrew Rehabilitation Center for Aged, 1200 Center Street, Roslindale, Massachusetts 02131.

NEEDS OF THE ELDERLY

What do we know about the needs of these older Americans? Old age can be a time of continued well-being and activity. However, it is true that the old, especially those over 75, are more likely to suffer from disease and disability, and therefore to utilize doctors, health and related services more often,[3] and to be more vulnerable to institutionalization than any other age cohort in our society. It has been estimated from data from the 1979 and 1980 National Health Interview Survey that about 2.7 million of those 65 or over living in the community need functional assistance from another person for selected personal care or home management activities—7 percent of the population between 65 and 74 years of age, 16 percent between 75 and 84, and 39 percent of the 85 and older age group.[4]

We also know that the definition of health status for this group is no easy matter. Most medical care systems regard health as the absence of disease. They focus on the diagnosis, treatment and prevention of major diseases in order to maintain health. However, for the elderly, especially the very elderly, the major illnesses are principally chronic and frequently multiple. Not all the disability seen in this group is traceable to classically-defined disease entities, and functional assessment is at least as important as disease definition.[2] The health status of this cohort cannot be understood except in the context of the aged individual's social support system, functional goals and physical living environment. It is important to recognize that the functional status of an individual depends not only on his own capacities, but on environmental expectations and conditions. A simple example is the elderly person with limited stamina. In a barrier-free environment with easy access to shopping and little need to carry heavy packages, such a person may function in an independent manner and have the residual energy not only to handle the necessary activities of daily living, but also to be an active member of the community. The same individual living on the third floor of an apartment building with no access to public transportation, located in a hilly terrain, who must walk a distance to shop will appear to have much lower functional status. Without help, such an individual may be exhausted by the effort and be unable to participate in community functions. Similarly, expectations and demands on the individual may affect performance.

The difficulties in maintaining older people in optimum condition are exacerbated by the structure and attitudes inherent in our health care system which, although it is excellent in many ways, lacks mechanisms for detection or early prevention efforts. This deficiency may adversely affect others in society as well, but it is an especially serious problem in the case of older people. The elderly often suffer from a cluster of illnesses, making it easy for one or another of their conditions to be overlooked. This difficulty is aggravated by stereotypes of aging which maintain that it is "natural" for older people to feel sick. This stereotype, unfortunately, is often accepted by older people themselves and causes them not to seek help when they are ill. Consequently, the passivity of the health system and the stereotypes of ageism can lead to instances where diseases progress undetected in elders, increasing the chances of prolonged disability and permanent functional losses. High risk elderly need to be identified and they need to be checked periodically for any rapid decline.

There are also special health needs among the elderly. One important example is the prevalence of iatrogenic disease in the over-65 group. An iatrogenic disease is one that is caused by an attempted cure, often by a drug. In terms of medical regimes, the elderly in our population use far more prescription drugs than does any other age group.[5] Older people frequently suffer from a combination of diseases or from chronic conditions, such as arthritis, that require prolonged medication. Therefore, they may be treated with a greater variety of drugs and/or take these drugs for longer periods of time than younger adults. In addition to this intensive use, the elderly often metabolize drugs more slowly than do their younger counterparts, a circumstance that increases the potential for adverse drug reactions and drug-drug interactions. Reactions to certain drugs may even result in confusion and hallucinatory states that can be mistaken for senility. These problems may be compounded still further because the elderly person and his/her family may be unaware of the potential for drug-induced iatrogenic illness.

Clearly, then, there is a need for understanding, advocacy and service provision for older people. Some of this support comes from the formal support system; however, spiralling costs and escalating pressures on governmental resources from all segments of our society make it obvious that the already overburdened formal system cannot cope with the expanding demand.

The challenge of restructuring society's approach to the delivery of long term care services without loss of quality of care has led many people to look more closely at how the informal support resource pool—family, friends and neighbors—responds to the need of the elderly for medical supervision and other nonmedical support such as shopping, transportation, meal preparation, housekeeping, and personal care. Data from numerous studies carried out in the recent past testify to the extensiveness of informal resource helping patterns.[6-22] As has often been demonstrated, formal services provide only a fraction of the needed help for the elderly in most noninstitutional settings, and informal sources play the crucial role in maintaining impaired elderly in the community.[11,23] The ability of the vulnerable elderly to live within the community appears to depend as much on the degree of personal isolation and the availability of effective helpers as it does on the individual's own level of functioning.[24]

There is, perhaps, an impression that families are negligent in this area, and that older people are forced to manage alone, abandoned by thankless children. A great deal of research, including our own, has found little truth to this bleak picture. Our data indicate that, so far at least, the pressures of contemporary life have not caused family ties to unravel. In fact, children and other family are primary sources of care for dependent community-residing elderly across race and ethnic groups, and family involvement with older members is extensive.[10,16-21] Even when one considers kin relationships for the 20 percent of the older population who have no children, contacts among family members are high.

Studies have shown that, for impaired elderly living alone, adult children are the major social support. One estimate indicates that families provide up to 80 percent of all home health care for all elderly individuals in need of such support.[25] The family's role in the provision of needed care has been identified as being significant for between 60-85 percent of the disabled in our society.[26]

FAMILY AS INFORMAL SUPPORTS

Highlighting the importance of the family as a source of informal support, it is estimated that for every severely impaired elderly person in an institution, there are at least two equally impaired elderly persons in the community; the major discriminating characteristic of those in the community is help from families.[27] In fact, those without kin who enter institutions are likely to be *less* impaired than those entering an institution who have families.[25,28,29] The importance of family relationships is also suggested by the fact that 20 percent of the nursing home population has no relatives, 86 percent no spouse—three times as many as in the general population—and studies have shown that those who are single, separated, divorced or widowed are more likely to become institutional residents.[30-32] Other research indicates that geographical separation from relatives is a factor contributing to institutionalization and that the most common events precipitating admission were the deaths or sudden illness of a close relative.[30,33]

Studies indicate that, even for families who do not see one another very often, at a time of need or with the onset of a disabling condition, there is a push to reconstitute close family relationships.[34,35] There is also evidence that most families want to help but that limitations to the degree of help provided arise because of other important obligations and environmental constraints.[36]

In a study conducted by the Department of Social Gerontological Research at the Hebrew Rehabilitation Center for Aged, in which the impact of a home care services program was evaluated,[12] we found that the informal support system was providing the bulk of the care for many sample members, especially in those cases where there would be a real danger of institutionalization were such help not available. Indeed, it was judged by the clinical assessors involved in this study that, were it not for the services provided by the family, 48 percent of the sample members might be institutionalized.

In a more recent study by our Department, the issue of informal support resiliency was analysed for a sample of 700 vulnerable elderly persons representing a broad spectrum of older people in the community, most of whom lived alone.[37] We found that this informal support network was strong and resilient in 58 percent of the cases, and for the majority of elderly and adult long term care populations, informal supports were the major source of nonmedical and medical supervision assistance. Moreover, there is a level of communication and caring such that the impaired elderly can count on their help without having to ask for it directly. The majority of vulnerable elderly people could count on at least one and usually more than one informal helper. It was extremely rare for there to be only formal resources (3%) or primarily formal resources (5%). Rather, for most of the vulnerable elderly in this study, formal supports served to fill gaps left by informal supports; it was the informal supports that provided the majority of services. The informal helpers addressed not only the existing needs of the elderly person, but also established a communication web that guaranteed that the helpers have the information on which to base changes in their helping behaviors as the individual's needs change over time.

In this study and others, in the event that children and other relatives were not available, friends and neighbors have stepped in to provide assistance. Friendship networks can effectively complement kin networks. For a large proportion of the elderly, informal support networks—whether family alone or complemented by others in the community—carry out a variety of helping tasks.

The family does provide considerable assistance. Nevertheless, given the magnitude of the problem, there is a need to develop other types of support. The family may be managing—perhaps heroically—to maintain their elderly relatives in the community, but the level at which they are able to maintain them may not be the optimum one. Also, it has been demonstrated that adding services from other sources does not generally cause the family to withdraw their help or reduce the amount of time spent with the elderly person. Instead, they often provide a different kind of help. Thus, if some of the routine chores were taken over by others, family members might have more time to simply enjoy and share pleasures with their older relatives.

Family members, however, are not always able to provide services that are needed. Coping with the often simple needs of the impaired elderly person—help with shopping or picking up mail, for instance—can become a problem because of the mobility of our society. There is at least some evidence that major exchanges between helper and helpee occur with those who live close to one another.[38] Geographic proximity seems to be more important than blood relationship. Those who are separated from potential helpers by mobility and distance may have significant unmet needs that prevent them from living a full life. Furthermore, there are pockets of impaired elderly people who have little or no informal help. Many of these individuals do not become institutionalized, but they live in the community at an unacceptable level—for example, the lonely elderly man who finds it difficult to shop and cook and who lives for weeks at a time on little more than crackers and tea.

THE ROLE OF THE CHURCH

Traditionally, the Church has extended a hand of fellowship to its members, binding families together into one larger family. Church members have helped the Church and one another and have been helped in their turn. The Church can build on this sense of community and of connectedness in order to stimulate and to provide additional informal supports to the vulnerable elderly within their faith community.

For example, the Church can play an advocacy role. It can disseminate information about health, nutrition and available services so that the elderly and/or their primary caretakers can do a more effective job. If necessary, it can play a direct advocacy role when the family is absent or needs help. An example of the effectiveness of an advocacy role can be seen, for example, in our study of the highly successful Pennsylvania Domiciliary Care program.[39] This was a program designed to serve two other target populations in addition to chronically ill and impaired aged—mental health, and mental retardation clients, although large numbers of persons over 60 years of age were found in these two groups as well. The program placed persons primarily in small family-type foster homes that provided personal care services, 24-hour supervision when necessary, and the normal range of meal, laundry, and other household services. We found that persons currently in long term care institutions—in particular, the institutionalized mental health applicants—were more likely to be placed if they had children nearby. While the children of applicants were seemingly unable to provide their parents with homes and supportive services themselves, it is reasonable to surmise that they acted effectively on their behalf as intercessors with the domiciliary care agency. In the absence of families able to play this role, the church could step in and provide advocacy support for elderly or handicapped people in the community.

It should be remembered also that the elderly, even the vulnerable elderly, can give as well as receive. Helping others is an important form of human communication, and altruism may contribute to feelings of self-esteem and psychological well-being. This is true for those who are in long term care institutions as well as others. Traditionally, nursing home residency fosters dependence, so it can be especially important for the institutionalized elderly to engage in useful activity, in order to stimulate independence and social involvement. An example of an initiative in which nursing home residents enrich their own lives by helping others is a Foster Grandparents Program, developed at the Hebrew Rehabilitation Center for Aged in Boston by social worker Joyce K. desRoches, ACSW. desRoches was later joined in this effort by nurse clinician Katharine Murphy, MSN. As desRoches and Murphy explain in their paper "Stimulating Independence in the Institutionalized Elderly Through a Foster Grandparent Group,"[40] the program evolved from a support discussion group led by desRoches, composed primarily of ambulatory residents with a range of auditory, visual and other impairments. When one of the members died and left a mentally retarded grandson to whom she was devoted, the members of the discussion group decided to adopt this orphaned 38-year-old, and have him visit them monthly at the Center. This was the beginning of a Foster Grandparents Program that eventually "adopted" two other mentally retarded adults who also visit monthly. By forming this group for the purpose of providing a community service, the focus of these elderly people is off themselves, diminishing the resident "sick role." In addition, the members are enthusiastic about being involved in a meaningful project.

Members of the group capitalize on their strengths rather than submitting to their limitations. For example, there are two secretaries for the group, one has a serious hearing deficit, the other cannot see or write. Together, they compensate and provide weekly minutes for the meetings. Group members say they feel less disabled, and appear more competent and optimistic as a result of participating in the group.

It may be that the Church should consider implementing such programs in some of its long term care facilities.

The Church can also provide a vehicle for parishioners to help one another. For example, the social ministry committee of a congregation might organize specific outreach programs for the elderly in the community. Programs of this type that are already being used by some churches include a person-to-person calling service in which older parishioners are called and asked about their health and well-being. Meals-on-wheels or friendly visitor programs are other examples.

AN ALTERNATIVE TO STIMULATING INFORMAL CARE

Also, in addition to the initiatives to foster and stimulate informal supports already mentioned, there is another, as yet untried, initiative—encourage a volunteer support network that will improve the quality of life of our older citizens and promote the welfare of the community as a whole. The concept of this initiative was developed by Ruth C. Weiner, Volunteer Services Coordinator for the Rhode Island Department of Social and Rehabilitative Services and myself. A similar idea has also been proposed by Professor Alan Sagar of Boston University.[41]

Although it is a new program, the idea behind it is an old one. We find it in Proverbs 27:10 which reads, in part, "Forsake not your father or your father's friend . . . better a neighbor who is close than a friend who is far off."

In our highly mobile society, brothers are often far off, as are children and other family members. What if, by helping an elderly neighbor in your town with, for example, shopping or meal preparation, you could not only do a good deed but also earn credits to be used later by your elderly parent living far away, or you could accumulate and use such credits yourself when you are older? Such credits could also be gathered and then shared as a gift to those in need.

This is the concept, similar to the one used by the Red Cross Blood Bank, behind what we call the *Samaritans' Cooperative Bank*. It is a plan that has the potential to help older people remain in the community, and it also could provide assistance to families who, as I pointed out earlier, are already doing a tremendous amount to care for their older members and who could certainly use assistance. They would get real help, and they would also gain the emotional support of knowing that they are not alone. It could also provide peace of mind for many people who would know that they could give of their time today and be assured of help tomorrow should they need it. This program would also be useful for those who wish to exchange time; for example, someone who works during the day and cannot care for an elderly parent but who could donate time on weekends or in the evening could exchange credits with someone who could help during the day but needs evenings and weekends free. This type of exchange will become increasingly important as more women work outside the home and are unavailable to provide care during working hours.

This program will never and is not intended to replace formal services. Formal services will still have to be provided to the vulnerable elderly population. However, it is known that it is the informal support network that is really the heart of long term care for our older citizens. The formal system has neither adequate manpower nor adequate financing available to replace informal services. Nor would that really be appropriate even if it were possible. Many kinds of help, such as friendly visiting, are more suitably given by the informal rather than the formal support network. The Samaritans' Cooperative Bank would supplement the formal and informal supports already in place with more informal assistance.

An organized and geographically widespread group such as a religious denomination is an ideal coordinator for such a volunteer program. The community concept that underlies the plan is already part of the fabric of church life. Moreover, the church has well-developed lines of authority and communication that would be invaluable resources both in designating and developing a workable system of credits and determining what value would be assigned to what type of service. It might be the responsibility of the social ministry committee to decide, for instance, whether more difficult or unpleasant tasks would be given a higher worth than less onerous assignments. The well-defined church organization would also be helpful in setting up a central data base to keep records of services rendered and received. Also, the church's history of outreach would make it easier to help members of the congregation actively target those frail elderly who are in need of services, and convince those individuals to accept assistance.

The potential help that could be offered through the Samaritans' Bank would include a whole range of services including transportation to doctor's appointments or to stores, recreational activities or places of worship; meal preparation or meals-on-wheels; respite care for families so that, for instance, a family could take a vacation secure in the knowledge that their elderly relative would be cared for; having an elderly person who is alone as a guest at Christmas or Easter is another possible service, as is reading to a blind person or doing heavy tasks such as yard work or snow shoveling. Just being a friend to an elderly person by interesting them in activities or helping them to continue with old hobbies is yet another service that could be provided through the Samaritans' Bank. It is to be hoped that the Samaritans' Cooperative Bank, like the informal support network already in place, will respond to the needs of the people involved and will provide a wide spectrum of services for the vulnerable elderly.

There are many possible advantages of such a program. For one thing, as Professor Sagar points out in his article on the possibility of a mutual aid bank,[41] time is more equitably distributed than money across lines of class and race, and its use does not require taxation, legislation or large administrative overheads. Also, help given this way is less likely to be regarded as unwelcome "charity" and rejected. If your mother in Iowa City knows that the man who shovels her snow is earning credits that will be used to provide transportation help for his father in California, she is less likely to feel like the object of charity and more likely to feel like a part of a living community. At the same time, the man who volunteers to shovel the snow will be able to actively help his parent without traveling hundreds of miles and disrupting his life to do so. It seems clear that the future will present many challenges in long term care. Large numbers of elderly and a scarcity of resources will mean that effective alternative methods of caring for the nation's vulnerable older citizens will have to be found. The Samaritans' Cooperative Bank takes the old American values of simple neighborliness and mutual help and expands them to meet the demands of contemporary life. Families do a great deal, but they need help especially in a country as large and as mobile as this one. This exchange bank is one possible way of mobilizing such help. The Church could be a pioneer in developing this long term care initiative. Later, if it is successful, the *Samaritans' Cooperative Bank* could be used as a model for unions and other national organizations.*

REFERENCES

1. Dans, P.E. and M.R. Kerr, "Gerontology and Geriatrics in Medical Education," *New England Journal of Medicine*, 300: 228, 1979.
2. Campion, E.W., *Age Trends in Health Status*. Paper prepared as part of materials for Section 3.2, Health and Health Care Systems, background paper for the 1981 White House Conference on Aging.
3. Institute of Medicine, *The Elderly and Functional Dependency*, Washington, DC: National Academy of Sciences, 1977.
4. Feller, B., "Need for Care among Noninstitutionalized Elderly," in *Health, United States: 1983* [DHHS Publication No. (PHS) 84-1232], Washington, DC: U.S. Government Printing Office, 1983.
5. Besdine, R. and S. Sherwood, "Health Care Needs of Elderly in Congregate Housing," in *Congregate Housing for Older People: A Solution for the 1980's*, R.D. Chellis, J.F. Seagle, Jr., and B.M. Seagle, eds., Lexington, MA: Lexington Books, 1982.
6. Shanas, E., *Family Relationships of Older People*, Chicago: Health Information Foundation, 1961.
7. Sussman, M.B., "Relationships of Adult Children with Their Parents in the United States," in *Social Structure and the Family-Generational Relationships*, E. Shanas and G. Streib, eds., Englewood Cliffs, NJ: Prentice-Hall, 1965.
8. Jackson, J.J., "Comparative Life Styles and Family and Friend Relationships Among Older Black Women," *Family Coordinator*, 21(4):477-485, 1972.
9. Shimkin, D.B., E.M. Shimkin, and D.A. Frate, "The Extended Family in Black Societies," in *Handbook of Aging and the Social Sciences*, R. Binstock and E. Shanas, eds., New York: Van Nostrand Reinhold Co., 1976.

*Those who would like more information about this idea are invited to write to Dr. Sherwood at the Hebrew Rehabilitation Center for Aged, 1200 Centre Street, Roslindale MA 02131 or to Ruth Weiner, SRS, 111 Fountain Street, Providence, RI 02903.

10. U.S. General Accounting Office, Comptroller of the U.S., *The Well-Being of Older People in Cleveland, Ohio,* Report to the Congress, GAO-13-HRD-77-70, April, 1977.

11. Sherwood, S., J.N. Morris, C.E. Gutkin, and C.N. Wieners, "The Needs of Elderly Community Residents of Massachusetts" (mimeo), Boston: Department of Social Gerontological Research, Hebrew Rehabilitation Center for Aged, 1977. A final contract report for study supported by research contract with the Survey Research Program, University of Massachusetts, in connection with AoA Grant #90-A-641-01.

12. Gurland, B., L. Dean, R. Gurland, and D. Cook, "Personal Time Dependency in the Elderly of New York City," in *Dependency in the Elderly of New York City,* Community Council of Greater New York, ed., New York: Authors, 1978.

13. Cantor, M., "Neighbors and Friends," *Research on Aging,* 1(4), December, 1979.

14. Sussman, M., "Social and Economic Supports and Family Environment for the Elderly." Final report to the Administration on Aging, AoA Grant No. 90-A-316, January, 1980.

15. Morris, J.N., "Massachusetts Elderly: Their Vulnerability and Need for Support Services and the Role of the Commonwealth's Home Care Corporations," Boston: Department of Social Gerontological Research, Hebrew Rehabilitation Center for Aged, April, 1982. A final contract report for study supported by a contract with Department of Elder Affairs.

16. Seelbach, W.C., "Filial Responsibility and Morale Among Elderly Black and White Urbanites: A Normative and Behavioral Analysis," Doctoral Dissertation. University Park, PA: The Pennsylvania State University, Department of Sociology, 1976.

17. Black, D., "The Older Person and the Family," in *Aging: Prospects and Issues,* R. Davis, ed., Los Angeles: Ethel Percy Andrus Center, University of Southern California, 1973, 69-78.

18. Hays, W.C. and C.H. Mindel, "Extended Kin Relations in Black and White Families," *Journal of Marriage and the Family,* 35:51-57, 1973.

19. Mindel, C.H. and R.W. Habenstein, *Ethnic Families in America: Patterns and Variations,* New York: Elsevier Scientific Publishing Co., 1976.

20. Mayer, M.J., *Kin and Neighbors: Differential Roles in Differing Cultures.* Paper presented at the 29th Annual Gerontological Society Scientific Meeting, New York, New York, 1976.

21. Shanas, E., "Social Myth as Hypothesis: The Case of the Family Relations of Old People," *Gerontologist,* 19(1):3-9, 1979.

22. Shanas, E., P. Townsend, H. Wedderburn, P. Friis, M. and J. Stenhouwer, *Old People in Three Industrial Societies,* Salem, NH: Ayer Co., 1968.

23. Shanas, E., "Measuring the Home Health Needs of the Aged in Five Countries," *Journal of Gerontology,* 26(1):37-40, 1971.

24. Kahana, E. and R.M. Coe, "Alternatives in Long Term Care," in *Long Term Care: A Handbook for Researchers, Planners and Providers,* S. Sherwood, ed., Englewood Cliffs, NJ: Spectrum, 1975.

25. Brody, S.J., W. Poulshock and C.F. Masciocchi, "The Family Caring Unit: A Major Consideration in Long Term Support," *Gerontologist,* 18:556-561, 1978.

26. Callahan, J.J., Jr., L. Diamond, J. Giele, and R. Morris, "Responsibility of Families for Their Severely Disabled Elders," *Health Care Financing Review,* 1(3):29-48, 1980.

27. Shanas, E., "The Family as a Social Support System in Old Age," *Gerontologist,* 19 (2):169-174, 1979.

28. York, J. and R.J. Calsyn, "Family Involvement in Nursing Homes," *Gerontologist,* 17(6):500-505, 1977.

29. Barney, J., "The Prerogative of Choice in Long Term Care," *Gerontologist,* 17: 309-314, 1977.

30. Townsend, P., "The Effects of Family Structure on the Likelihood of Admission to an Institution in Old Age: The Application of General Theory," in *Social Structure and the Family,* E. Shanas and G. Streib, eds., Englewood Cliffs, NJ: Prentice-Hall, 1965.

31. Gottesman, L.E., "Nursing Home Performance as Related to Resident Traits, Ownership, Size and Source of Payment," *American Journal of Public Health,* 64: 1974.

32. Beattie, W.M. and J. Bullock, *Preface for a Counseling Service: A Study of 1,085 Residents of Nursing Homes and Homes for the Aged,* St. Louis: Health and Welfare Council of Metropolitan St. Louis, 1963.

33. Brody, E.M., "The Aging Family," *Gerontologist,* 6: 1966.

34. Blau, P.M., *Exchange and Power in Social Life,* New York: Wiley, 1964.

35. Sussman, M.B., "The Family Life of Old People," in *Handbook of Aging and the Social Sciences,* R. Binstock and E. Shanas, eds., New York: Van Nostrand Reinhold Co., 1976.

36. Maddox, G.L., "Families as Context and Resource in Chronic Illness," in *Long Term Care: A Handbook for Researchers, Planners and Providers,* S. Sherwood, ed., Englewood Cliffs, NJ: Spectrum, 1975.

37. Morris, J.N. and S. Sherwood, "Informal Support Resources for Vulnerable Elderly Persons: Can They Be Counted On, Why Do They Work?" *International Journal of Aging and Human Development,* 18(2):81-98, 1983/84.

38. Sussman, M.B., "The Isolated Nuclear Family: Fact or Fiction?" *Social Problems,* 6: 1959.

39. Sherwood, S., J.N. Morris and C.E. Gutkin, "Evaluation of Pennsylvania's Domiciliary Care Pilot Program," Boston: Department of Social Gerontological Research, Hebrew Rehabilitation Center for Aged, 1981. A final report in connection with HEW Contract #130-76-12.

40. desRoches, J., and K. Murphy, *Stimulating Independence in the Institutionalized Elderly Through a Foster Grandparent Group.* Paper presented at the 4th Annual Northeastern Gerontological Society Meeting, Philadelphia, PA, April, 1984.

41. Sagar, A., "A Proposal for Promoting More Adequate Long Term Care for the Elderly," *The Forum,* 23(1):13-17, 1983.

Government Funding Treatment of Non-Profits Weakens Desired Results

Roger A. Rotvig, B.A., S.M.

ABSTRACT. Framers of public policy continually ask the voluntary sector to increase its response to social needs. Yet there are biases in fundamental social legislation that favor the profit making sector over the voluntary.

The results of such treatment are that the voluntary sector tends to concentrate its delivery on quality service at higher than average costs, relying on non-operating income to cover the gap between costs and charges. A second tendency is to gear services disproportionately to those able to pay full costs, making the provider less dependent on an inequitable public funding source.

TITLE XVIII AMENDMENTS

The original passage of Title XVIII of the Social Security Act (Medicare) in 1966 did not recognize a return on net capital equity as a reimbursable cost. In 1967, after considerable discussion, Congress amended the Act (Section 1861 (v) (1) (B)) expressly to provide proprietary facilities a reasonable return on equity capital as a necessary cost of operations. The amendment just as expressly denied such a return on equity capital for non-profit providers.

Subsequent enactment of Title XIX (Medicaid) built on the same capital equity decisions worked out in the 1967 amendment. A look at the issues that moved Congress to that 1967 amendment can clearly assist in defining both the problem and the solution that may enable the voluntary sector to assume its expected role as a major service deliverer, especially in the field of long term care of the aged, without regard to their ability to pay.

Roger A. Rotvig is President, Lutheran Service Association of New England, 74 Sherman Street, Hartford, Connecticut 06105.

The key Congressional hearing at which this philosophy was hammered out took place before the Senate Finance Committee on May 25, 1966. The proposed Medicare reimbursement formula for Title XVIII had been published on May 2, 1966, and certain elements in the formula had triggered an outcry that sent Congress back to the drawing board on this issue that was ultimately adjusted in the above mentioned 1967 amendment to Title XVIII. Senator Russell Long of Louisiana chaired the meeting. Other senators present were George Smathers of Florida, Clinton Anderson of New Mexico, Paul Douglas of Illinois, Herman Talmadge of Georgia, Abraham Ribicoff of Connecticut, John Williams of Delaware, Frank Carlson of Kansas and Carl Curtis of Nebraska.[1]

Three important bits of testimony were considered that day: one, the Senate Finance Committee staff report presented by Mr. Jay Constantine; a second, a lengthy statement by Mr. Robert Ball, Commissioner of Social Security, who was assisted by Mr. Robert Myers, Chief Actuary; the third was a 41 page report reviewing the principles of reimbursement by the Comptroller General, Mr. Elmer Staats.

UNIQUE TESTIMONY ON CAPITAL EQUITY

Except for the Finance Committee staff report, overwhelming unanimity was given to the principle that the non-profit and the profit making provider should be treated equally with regard to a return on equity being seen as a reimbursable cost. The committee staff report presented that day urged that it be denied to non-profit providers and this position was eventually written into the amendment and persists in almost the same form to this day. The most relevant bits of testimony are recorded below.

The Commissioner of Social Security, Mr. Ball, used a recommendation of Health Insurance Benefits Council, a group created by Federal law, to make his first point on equal treatment of providers. He stated in part: The majority of the council believe that any inclusion in the cost of an allowance for the use of money should apply equally to non-profit organizations and profit making organizations alike.[2] Later in his testimony, Mr. Ball asked to have inserted into the record the five page memorandum of the Chief Counsel to the Social Security Administrator, Mr. Alanson Willcox. The memo, dated May 24, 1966, includes a full airing of the implications of treating non-profit and profit making providers differently. Key sections read as follows:

> As has been said, a strong argument was made for the inclusion of a factor for equity capital of all providers, proprietary and nonprofit alike, the decisive argument to the contrary being the cost of such a provision and the lack of indication that its inclusion was contemplated by Congress. Inclusion of this item for proprietary institutions alone would obviously cost very much less. In the case of new construction, indeed, recognition of profit might in large part lead merely to a different form of financing at no greater cost to the Government.
>
> Despite these considerations, however, it is extremely difficult to rationalize a difference of treatment in this regard between profit and nonprofit institutions. The Secretary may not pay more than cost, and under the classical dichotomy this means that he may not contribute to a profit. He may, it is true, determine costs "for various types or classes of institutions," but this authority does not exempt him, with respect to any type or class, from the overriding limitation that he may pay only the reasonable cost . . . To make the distinction suggested would involve the Secretary, as it seems to me, in a logical contradiction. He would have to say to the nonprofit institutions that the cost of the use of capital (even without any return for risk-taking) is an element of profit and not of cost, but say to the proprietary institutions that—because they are organized in the hope of profit—this same item is in their case an element of cost and not of profit.[3]

The Comptroller General of the United States, Mr. Staats, was not present at the hearing but his cover letter to his 41 page report indicated that he was responding to prior requests of the Finance Committee to review these unresolved issues. After discussing this return on equity issue, he writes:

> If nonprofit medical institutions are viewed as operating on a static basis, with no element of growth or increasing sophistication in facilities and equipment involved, a return above actual costs in the traditional accounting sense would not be appropriate. But these institutions cannot operate statically if

they are to provide the kind and level of medical services on a continuing basis to which patients should be entitled. There is a constant need for additional capital to keep pace with medical advancements. In practice, this additional capital is provided through donations and borrowings. Theoretically, at least, it would not seem unreasonable to conclude that charges to patients should contain an element toward meeting this need for continual capital accretion. And in this context, it would further seem reasonable to construe a charge toward meeting this need as a "reasonable cost" of providing medical services. . . .

Capital is used whether it is owned or borrowed, and a return on equity for the nonprofit institution at least has the virtue of retaining the funds involved in the sphere of improving the quality or quantity of available medical care, whereas interest costs and return on equity for profit institutions which are paid are lost to the medical complex.[4]

The Committee of the Senate Finance Committee submitted a 37 page report, 15 of which related directly to the question, can reasonable cost include a return on investment for proprietary institutions without similar payment to non-profit facilities?[5] Staff conclusions were:

In the opinion of staff, justification exists both in the statute itself and the accompanying actuarial concept of what constitutes reasonable cost for the payment of an appropriate return on capital to proprietary institutions without similar authorizations for non-profit facilities.[6]

AN ANALYSIS OF THE WEIGHT OF TESTIMONY

It is hard to read the various strong statements by the Commissioner of Social Security Administration, its General Counsel, the Comptroller General and the Health Insurance Benefits Advisory Council and realize that their unanimous position was overruled by the Finance Committee on the basis of their staff recommendation.

Tax exemption is the first reason for such a recommendation. The staff refers to this as an advantage that proprietaries do not have, contributing to the need for some other equalizing factor. However, the proprietary provider can include all of his taxes as a part of his reasonable cost in the establishment of his reimbursement rate. Another reason given for the differential treatment is the fact that a large portion of voluntary facilities were built with Hill Burton grants or other donated monies. The Staff testimony focused on the Hill Burton issue and described this as the government giving the equity and then paying a return on it through the years. This factor may have been true to some extent in the case of hospitals in 1966 but it never was a major factor in long term care. In any regard, a simple exemption could have been placed in any reimbursement formula so that a return would not apply to that portion of equity attributed to a Hill Burton Grant.

Finally, the Staff report stated their third reason for the differential of treatment. It was that non-profit institutions do not expect to make a profit.

It appears reasonable to assume that nonprofit institutions would expect to be reimbursed only for their normal costs of providing care. They are not ordinarily paid a return on investment.[7]

Staff appears to be using economic situations of the '50s and early '60s as a planning tool for the last third of the century. With life-safety regulations, new staffing and service requirements and efficiency demands which usually come only with increased size, the non-profit provider needed to undergo extensive expansions and had to go to commercial borrowing sources since contributions of the size and at the time required were seldom available and no equity return was available as a source of additional investment.

THE EFFECTS OF DIFFERENT TREATMENT ON RETURN ON EQUITY

While each state has developed an individual way of implementing the prohibition against a return on equity for non-profits, each has the same overall penalizing effect on a non-profit attempting to serve a high percentage of medicaid residents. The following is how Massachusetts would treat two identical four million dollar programs, one owned and operated by a non-profit, the other by a proprietary provider.

Costs

Cost of land $300,000—non depreciable
Cost of building $3,700,000—40 year depreciation (limited furnishings and mechanicals are accelerated)
Total project cost $4,000,000
Owner equity $800,000—20%
Borrowed at 12% for 15 years $3,200,000
Resident Mix: 80% medicaid 20% private

Treatment

First year interest payment of $384,000 × 80% amounts to $307,200 available equally to profit making and non-profit providers. Interest amount decreased equally to both each year as capital repayment progresses.

Level depreciation payments of $92,500 × 80% amounts to $74,000 available to both class of provider. (First ten years are slightly higher and last 30 slightly lower due to variable accelerated depreciation allowances.)

A return on equity of $70,400 is paid to the profit making provider in the first year. This amount will change as equity changes (capital repayments added, repairs and improvements added, 2 1/2% depreciation deducted annually). The non-profit provider receives none of this payment. First year equity is $800,000 × 11% = $88,000 × 80% = $70,400.

Local property taxes estimated at $36,000 are not charged to a non-profit provider and the profit making provider recovers 80% of it, or $28,800 in the rate based on approved costs of operation.

Summary

First year income available to the profit making provider from medicaid sources: $307,200 + $74,000 + $70,400 total $451,600.

First year income available to the non-profit provider from medicaid sources: $307,200 + $74,000 total $381,200.

The proprietary provider has $70,400 more to cover the fixed costs. As equity in the property increases either by larger initial capital payments (lower borrowing) or by natural or accelerated capital ownership or by repairs and additions being added out of non-borrowed sources, the equity income difference between the two types of providers increases.

POLICY DECISIONS FLOWING
FROM RETURN ON EQUITY ISSUES

It can be forcefully argued that the Senate Finance Committee's efforts to contain costs in their 1967 actions have forced non-profit providers to make fundamental policy choices as they respond to long term care needs.

One choice is to lessen their dependence on an inequitable medicaid system by building facilities that cater to those able to pay for care. This generally means more space and more luxury than medicaid standards allow, but those able to pay generally expect this. A reduction in the mix from 80% medicaid and 20% private (the national average) to 50-50 will make the inequity of payment described in the above section far more manageable.

Another choice, made by those who decide to serve their share of the medicaid residents, is to have significantly higher than average financing costs for the next 40 years. With the primary source of capital repayment coming from a 40 year depreciation schedule and with the reality that few commercial loans can be found for longer than 15 years, there will be a strong reason to re-finance periodically, keeping interest costs high and capital ownership low. Unlike the profit making provider, there is no incentive, only penalties, to hasten the transfer of equity from the bank to the provider.

WHAT THE FUTURE HOLDS

There needs ultimately to be an informed and concerted effort on the part of non-profit providers in the field of care for the aging as well as other service areas, to convince government policy makers of the shortsightedness of policies such as those formed by the Title XVIII amendments.

An opening in the process exists now and non-profit providers need to impact on the reimbursement procedures that are currently evolving. On January 18, 1984, H.H.S. implemented regulations on the ''Boren Amendment to the 1980 Omnibus Reconciliation Act.'' The effect of the amendment and subsequent regulations is to give states almost complete authority over medicaid reimbursement issues while retaining full federal control over medicare. Thus individualized state plans to respond to non-profit return on equity needs will no longer be reversed by federal regulations citing the

1967 action, even though that specific exemption of return on equity for non-profits still exists.

State reimbursement regulation writers, in their various conditions of enlightenment, are free to do what they wish. We have heard of examples of proposed state responses to allow one-third of the return on equity for a non-profit provider as they would for a profit maker. Another state considered allowing 90% of what a proprietary provider would get, but then abandoned that plan. Most states are considering no changes in this policy.

WHAT CAN BE DONE?

Non-profit providers in every state ought to analyze the current reimbursement regulations in their state to determine the implications of the "return on equity" issue to them. A good way to do this is to prepare a comparative study of two equal facilities as has been done previously in this paper.

Another study worth undertaking by the non-profit provider is to recalculate one's fixed cost reimbursement if one moved from one's present medicaid/private patient mix (often 40-60 for non-profits) to the current national average of 80-20.

Church leaders at the judicatory level who participate in the endorsement process of Long Term Care Facilities ought to learn the patient mix facts of their homes and determine to what extent these facts agree with their understanding of the mission of the church and to what extent adjustments can be made in the light of fixed cost regulations of medicaid such as the return on equity issue.

National church leadership and staff should engage in the collection of information that delineates the extent to which the various state practices treat non-profits unequally in regard to capital and fixed costs and to what extent the philosophy of service has been skewed by these medicaid practices.

Each participant, the non-profit provider, the judicatory official and the national church leadership and staff should mount campaigns before the state legislatures, the medicaid regulatory body and the U.S. Congress to have these unequal treatment provisions, and their unfortunate consequences, rewritten. Whatever else one might believe about the outcome, as the Controller General stated in his testimony, ". . . a return on equity for the non-profit institution at least has the virtue of retaining the funds involved in the sphere of improving the quality and quantity of available medical care . . ."

NOTES

1. *Reimbursement Guidelines for Medicare.* Hearing before the Committee on Finance, United States Senate, May 25, 1966. U.S. Government Printing Office (1966) p. 1.
2. Ibid., page 48.
3. Ibid., page 93.
4. Ibid., page 149.
5. Ibid., page 27.
6. Ibid., page 34.
7. Ibid., page 33.

The Rural Elderly
and the Church

Graham D. Rowles, Ph.D.

ABSTRACT. The growing numbers of rural elderly in America
has resulted in a burgeoning of research on this constituency. Such
research has identified information on the living circumstances of
rural elderly as well as on the advantages and disadvantages of the
rural milieu as a context for aging. Research has also demonstrated
the central role which religion and the church play for the rural elderly, and it is with this knowledge that the church must expand its
role in service to this population. The church may enhance its role by
beginning with four major areas: (1) increasing church accessibility;
(2) complementing formal service programs; (3) enhancing indigenous support networks; and (4) providing educational programs.

Each Sunday, Audrey,[1] now 87 years old, watches her neighbors
leave for church.

> You know after you've gone to church all your life, it's hard
> not to be able to. I sit here and look out the window and watch
> them all go, and then I turn the TV on and listen. It's the next
> best thing . . . Sunday, I look out more because I'm watching
> people go to church. Since I can't go to church, I watch the
> cars go by, watch Jean and Conrad leaving, McCories, all of
> them . . . and then at noon, I watch them all come back.

When I first met her in 1978, Audrey was making the half-mile
trip herself. Her neighbors, Jean and Conrad, would give her a ride.
As she grew more frail, Audrey found it ever more difficult to climb

---

Graham D. Rowles is Associate Director for Social and Behavioral Sciences,
Multidisciplinary Center of Gerontology, Sanders-Brown Building, University of Kentucky, Lexington, Kentucky 40506-0027.

the stairs into the church and to endure an hour sitting on the wooden pews. So, she now participates vicariously. Religion has always been a central focus in Audrey's life. There is a sense of sometimes puzzled ("Why did he let an old thing like me live and take my son?") but generally unchallenged fatalism with regard to God's plan for her. Her faith and sense of implicit trust extends to the clergy. Such trust is all the more poignant in view of a succession of ministers at her church during the time I lived in Colton.[2] One individual, a soft-spoken man, left under a cloud shortly after his propensity for wife abuse became common knowledge. Another was a charlatan who had misrepresented his credentials and was not even an ordained minister!

Audrey is a member of a study panel with whom I have been engaged in ethnographic research for almost seven years (Rowles, 1980, 1981, 1983a,b,c, 1984). The panel originally comprised fifteen persons, ranging in age from 62 to 91 years, who lived in a rural Appalachian community of 403 persons. Through my interaction with these people I gained some insight into growing old in this particular setting and into the role religion and the church play in enhancing the experience for the elderly and their families. A number of illustrations in this paper are derived from this study.

WHO ARE THE RURAL ELDERLY?

Many scholars employ demographic criteria and, using a U.S. Bureau of the Census definition, restrict the term rural to communities of less than 2,500 persons. According to this criterion, in 1980, 6,497,620 persons (25.48% of the total elderly population) resided in rural areas. There is considerable variation among states in the proportion of the elderly population which is rural (Figure 1). The South, the Midwest and the Plains states reveal the highest percentages of rural elderly. However, the population of concern changes somewhat when we look at the numbers involved (Figure 2). Many of the more urbanized states in the north and east also contain the largest numbers of rural elderly. Focusing on a more local level, within some states there are a significant number of counties in which the elderly are 100% rural. For example, in West Virginia 18 of 55 counties contain no community with 2,500 residents.

Placing these data in temporal perspective illustrates demographic trends that became apparent during the 1970s when metropolitan

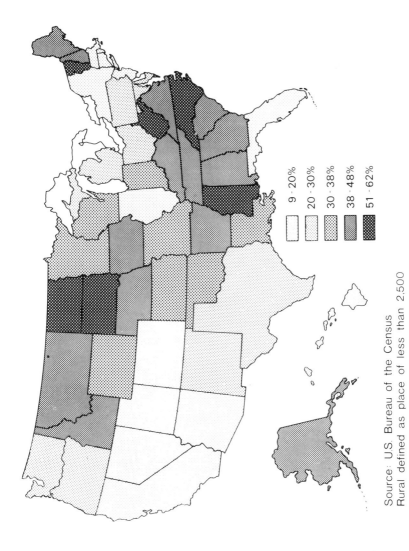

Source: U.S. Bureau of the Census
Rural defined as place of less than 2,500

9 - 20%
20 - 30%
30 - 38%
38 - 48%
51 - 62%

FIGURE 1. Percent of Elderly (65+) living in rural areas in 1980.

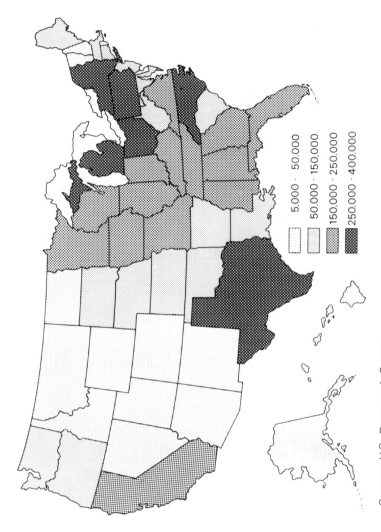

Source: U.S. Bureau of Census
Rural defined as place of less than 2,500

FIGURE 2. Number of rural elderly (65+) in 1980.

5,000 - 50,000
50,000 - 150,000
150,000 - 250,000
250,000 - 400,000

America began losing population to rural areas, especially to small towns. Between 1970 and 1980 the rural elderly population of the United States increased by over a million (from 5,434,387 to 6,497,620). In a number of states elderly populations that had "aged in place" were complemented by a stream of both return migrants and persons of urban birth desiring to retire to the countryside (Fuguitt and Tordella, 1980; Aday and Miles, 1982). There are growing concentrations of elderly people in rural areas as diverse as northern Michigan, western North Carolina, and the Ozarks region of Arkansas.

One outcome of these trends is an increasing need to distinguish among diverse rural elderly populations, often residing in a shared environment. On the one hand, are lifelong elderly residents who are fully assimilated into local culture and value systems. Often these people have developed an elaborate network of interpersonal relationships and mutual obligations within the community that serves as the foundation of an effective support system in their old age (Lozier and Althouse, 1974; Pihlblad, 1975; Rowles, 1980). On the other hand, are the new migrants. These old people are not attuned to the mores of rural life. They have not had time to develop relationships with other members of the community that can serve as a source of support. Often, they do not have an extensive kin network within the vicinity. Instead, they are socialized to an urban milieu of formal service programs and instrumental relationships.

On the local scale there may also be considerable variation within rural environments. The lifestyles and potential support networks of elderly people living in the center of a small town surrounded by homes are likely to be very different from those of their peers living on the outskirts or on isolated farmsteads. It is also important to acknowledge regional variations: Appalachian hollows, Texas rangelands, and rural Vermont provide contrasting settings in which to grow old.

Recent acknowledgement of the growing numbers of rural elderly has resulted in a burgeoning of research (for a recent review see Coward and Lee, 1984). What does this research tell us about the circumstances of the rural elderly?

GROWING OLD IN RURAL AMERICA

One of the more consistently reported findings is that the "objective" circumstances of the rural elderly are worse than their urban counterparts. Incomes are lower (Lee and Lassey, 1980). Housing is older, in inferior physical condition, and more likely to be lacking in basic facilities (Atchley and Miller, 1979; Bylund, Crawford and LeRay, 1979). Rural old people tend to be in poorer health and to have less access to health services (Konan, Tweed and Longest, 1979; McCoy and Brown, 1978). Many rural elderly have deficient diets (Glover, 1981). There is evidence that some rural elderly experience problems of loneliness (Kivett, 1979) and that others are geographically isolated from their children (Powers, Keith and Goudy, 1979; Rowles 1983a,b). Transportation is also a serious problem (McKelvey, 1979; Patton, 1975). Finally, most rural areas lack the array of service programs available to the urban elderly (Coward, 1979; Nelson, 1980; Taietz and Milton, 1979).

This gloomy scenario is somewhat alleviated by an important paradox. Despite inferior objective circumstances, the rural elderly do not score lower on measures of morale or life satisfaction than their urban peers. Indeed, studies employing a variety of measures, have indicated surprisingly high levels of subjective well-being (Donnenwerth, Guy and Norvell, 1978; Grams and Fengler, 1981; Hynson, 1976; Lee and Lassey, 1980).

There are two possible explanations for the paradox. First, many of the objective disadvantages of the rural elderly may be a function of the way we have chosen to measure disadvantage. Dollar income statistics may not adequately reflect resources. Eighty-two percent of all rural elderly housing units are owner occupied and, consequently, most rural elderly people pay no rent (Beall, Thompson, Godwin and Donahue, 1981). The rural elderly are far more likely to cultivate gardens and to own freezers (Atchley and Miller, 1979). Participation in the informal exchange economy of many rural environments also reduces costs. Finally, rural folk often have different perceptions of the meaning of income than do their urban counterparts (Grams and Fengler, 1981). For example, Coward and Kerckhoff (1978, p. 37) report research in which 91% of the rural elderly respondents considered their income to be "adequate."

A second explanation for the paradox is that rural settings are conducive to well-being and high morale in old age. Rural environments are less pervaded by the fear of crime that restricts the urban elderly, are characterized by a culture allowing more gradual transition to aged status and foster a socio-cultural milieu conducive to high levels of social participation and support for the elderly (Lee and Lassey, 1980). It is useful to focus on these and other aspects of rural environments that tend to be supportive for old people and to contrast these with residual problem areas.

THE RURAL MILIEU AS A CONTEXT FOR AGING

One advantage of rural residence is that the pace of physical change is often far slower than in the city. This makes it possible for the vulnerable person to use familiarity with the setting to compensate for slowed reaction times and failing cognitive abilities. The confidence this instills is further reinforced by the slower pace of life in rural areas (Bornstein, 1979).

Low population density and, in many areas, the tendency for population stability over time, are conducive to the development of a social milieu in which individuals are "known" and "know others." In Colton old people gain a sense of support from the knowledge that they are surrounded by people who know them and their family history (Rowles, 1983a). Local media, particularly the newspapers (via well read obituary columns) provide a constant source of reminders of individuals' affiliation with other community members. This sense of identification is reinforced during face-to-face meetings with age peers and is often a primary topic of conversation at the Senior Center or the church. The telephone is also a critical medium for reinforcing awareness networks. During one sample week in 1980, Audrey spent 11 hours 55 minutes talking on the telephone with age peers (Rowles, 1983a) (Figure 3.). This was not unusual. It was discovered that many panel members engaged in lengthy telephone conversations at a prearranged time each day. The existence and timing of these conversations was common knowledge in the community.

Looking more closely at the spatial pattern of telephone calls it became possible to see how they were a component of relatively localized indigenous support clusters of three or four elderly people living within the vicinity of each other. In Colton, and I suspect in most rural communities, there are many such clusters. Often the clusters are supported by younger people living nearby who provide both practical and emotional support. These people, frequently middle-aged women, will pick up groceries, bring in the mail from the roadside mailbox and perhaps even wash and set the hair of their elderly neighbors. They also provide rides to church or to the doctor's office. Indeed, these people sometimes become "surrogate" family for old people whose children have moved away.

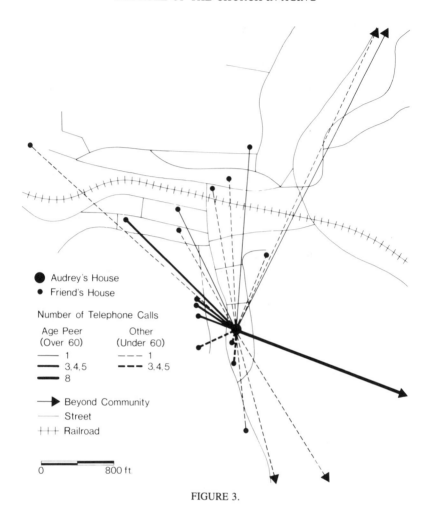

FIGURE 3.

Rural environments also present a variety of problems. Low population density means that a rural area may not have a large enough threshold population of individuals in need of a particular service to justify its provision. Even if a threshold population exists for a service, costs involved in providing adequate transportation are often prohibitive.

The spatial dispersion of old people in rural areas also presents dilemmas of isolation. Increasingly, the elderly of America are living alone. In 1980, 1,584,964 rural old people lived alone (U.S.

Bureau of the Census, 1980). In addition to difficulties this can generate in obtaining practical assistance, particularly in winter, there is the considerable potential for reinforcement of a sense of loneliness and abandonment.

A final problem is somewhat paradoxical. For some people the fact that everyone tends to be "known" and to know others can prove problematic. Newcomers tend to be considered "outsiders." Thus old people who move into rural communities may become unwittingly ostracized and feel somewhat alienated. A second aspect of the problem is that being well-known is fine if one is liked but can become a liability if one does not conform to local cultural norms and expectations.

It is within this context that the rural church must operate, sometimes as the sole source of support for its parishioners. How does the church fare? What role does it play within the lives of the rural elderly?

THE CURRENT ROLE OF THE CHURCH

According to Karcher and Karcher (1980, p. 410), "the single most important and trusted institution, outside of the family, in the lives of the rural elderly, is the church." Studies over several decades indicate extremely high levels of church membership among the rural elderly (Blazer and Palmore, 1976). Pihlblad and McNamara (1965) in their study of three small rural towns recorded a 90% level of church membership. In a more recent "panel" study of low income rural elderly, Stojanovic (1972) reported a similar figure. Finally, in her study of elderly rural Pennsylvania Germans, Collier found a 95% level of church membership (Collier, 1978).

High levels of membership translate into church attendance and participation. Pihlblad and McNamara (1965) found that 71% of the elderly were active in church activities. Collier (1978) discovered that 82% of her respondents attended church once a week or more and 88% attended at least twice a month. High participation levels are impressive in the context of the considerable distances traveled to church and reduced levels of involvement in other activities.

Religious participation among the elderly of rural America is not uniform. Collier's Pennsylvania study and my own work reveal that attendance at church related activities is significantly higher among women than men. The case of Beatrice and Walter, a married couple in my study who are in their mid-eighties, were born in houses a few yards apart and have never lived more than a mile from their present abode, provides a striking illustration. Each Sunday Walter drives Beatrice to church. He then returns home for an hour before retracing the half mile trip to pick her up at the conclusion of the service.

The importance of religion is also revealed in other domains. In Appalachia, reading the scriptures is a high priority daily activity. The topic of the sermon or other church related events are often the focus of conversations at the store or outside the post office. Indeed, the entire elderly community of Colton appears to be pervaded by a "religious ambience" (Collier, 1978, p. 44). As Collier concluded (Collier 1978, p. vii): "older people in the research population relate to each other, to the community, and in fact, to the aging experience through their religion." Finally, several studies have documented that church attendance and immersion within the ambience of the local religious community through contact with church related friends, is highly correlated with measures of well-being among the rural elderly (Ergood and Shelly, 1979; Ortega, Crutchfield and Rushing, 1983).

While the existence of a supportive "religious ambience" may be partially explained by the historical roots and traditions of many rural communities, it is important to acknowledge the role the contemporary church and the clergy play in maintaining this sense of christian community. In the absence of an extensive array of formal service programs, the church often serves as a locus for both religious and secular meetings. In addition, rural ministers play a critical part in sustaining the religious ambience of their parish through relationships they establish with parishioners and the image they project in their personal lives. My observations in Colton and surrounding communities indicate an almost embarrassingly high level of faith in "the minister." They also reveal the potential for schism, pettiness, and the collapse of local congregations, with a consequent loss of a critical source of support for their elderly members, when this level of trust is betrayed.

EXPANDING HORIZONS

Acknowledging the central role that religion and the church already play, what are the options for better serving the rural elderly? In seeking to explore fresh alternatives the church has important advantages. First, the trust and respect with which the clergy are invested can be harnessed to overcome a variety of barriers to providing assistance. Second, representatives of the church customarily possess a degree of moral authority that can be used to advantage. At the same time, it is necessary to acknowledge several constraints. Rural churches tend to be single minister parishes. They have neither the paid personnel and access to consultants nor the financial and informational resources available within many urban parishes that make possible innovative and capital intensive options currently pursued by the "corporate" church. In addition, as my observations on the individuals ministering to Audrey would indicate, rural parishes do not necessarily attract or retain the most able, experienced, creative or even desirable ministers.

Of course, there are many highly qualified and committed rural clergy for whom service within rural parishes is a vocation. However, there is a longstanding feeling that small rural parishes are entry level positions, stepping stones to larger urban or suburban parishes. If a rural parish is offered to an experienced pastor it is sometimes seen as exile or banishment. A number of factors contribute to this. Salaries in small parishes are low (even marginal). Since most rural parishes are small they have a continuing problem with offering salaries which would attract and retain pastors with experience or financial obligations such as a growing family. There is less opportunity for professional development, growth and networking. There are fewer opportunities for spouses and families in the areas of education, employment, culture and social life. The pastor must be a general practitioner since there are fewer formal support services for referral. The result is that the turnover for pastors in rural parishes is higher, the vacancies longer and the quality of pastoral care tends to be lower because rural parishes are a training ground and the understanding of rural culture and milieu is minimal. (Lucore, 1984)

In sum, there is a tendency for rural parishes to receive ministers who are either recent graduates from seminary who stay for a short period before moving on to more prestigious positions or, alternatively, individuals with more limited talents and aspirations.

Within the framework of these constraints, four important areas for enhancing the role of the church in the service of the rural elderly merit consideration.

Increasing Church Accessibility

The need to make rural churches physically accessible cannot be overemphasized, particularly in view of the importance the elderly attribute to attendance. The problem has three dimensions. First, is the problem of getting elderly people to church. This is particularly acute in rural areas because of the distances frequently involved. An informal network of ride providers already exists in many parishes. However, there are sometimes people who are by-passed by such ride sharing arrangements. A simple solution would be to form an ad hoc committee of church members whose assignment would be to ensure that all parishioners desiring to attend church are provided with rides. Many church members are willing to travel considerable distances out of their way to pick up an elderly parishioner.

A more serious dimension of the accessibility problem becomes apparent once the threshold of the church is reached. A surprisingly large number of rural churches present daunting barriers of poor environmental design (Stevenson, 1980; Kerr, 1980; Tilberg, 1984). These include steps that become dangerously slick when wet; long flights of stairs into the body of the church; the absence of handrails to provide support for those with an unsteady gait; poor lighting; inadequate heating or ventilation; inferior acoustics; and uncushioned pews that seem designed to ensure that people keep awake during the sermon. Some of these problems are not resolvable given the limited funds available to most churches. However, a simple survey of the design of the church, particularly with input from the elderly themselves, can result in significant improvements. An increase in the power of the lights on the stairs, the installation of handrails, and the placement of non-slip strips on steps, are all relatively inexpensive options that reduce the embarrassment many old people feel when they have to seek assistance in entering the church.

A final barrier is the duration of many church related events. Some old people no longer attend services because they simply cannot endure to sit for so long. Would it not be possible to have a short sermon officially scheduled at least once a month?

Complementing Formal Service Programs

A second area in which the church can enhance its contribution lies in complementing sparsely provided formal service programs.

High levels of church membership mean that the clergy provide an important conduit for disseminating information on programs and resources as they become available (Stojanovic, 1972, p. 259). Ministers might also assume a facilitating role in convening meetings of their congregation that serve as a forum for critically exploring the underlying value premises and theological bases of various service programs for the elderly (Flemming, 1984). In addition, ministers can play a crucial role in legitimating the use of services. The rural elderly are characteristically highly independent and reluctant to use formal services. Assurances from a trusted minister that participation in such programs is an entitlement rather than an expression of failure can often overcome psychological barriers to utilizing a needed service.

Several writers have suggested an even more active role in providing direct liaison with formal service programs. Dunckley and his associates provide an illustration of the way in which local ministers can be extremely helpful adjuncts within rural counseling and therapy programs:

> . . . one minister recently assisted us with an older woman who has a recurring history of admissions to the state hospital for depression. Each time a depressive episode occurred, the woman got angry and wanted to do harm to the people around her; she took this as evidence that she was being influenced by the devil. The woman was extremely passive and never expressed anger, even though there were numerous occasions in her life when it would have been appropriate. In therapy sessions we were unable to effectively counter her beliefs about the devil or work on getting the woman to express her anger in more productive ways. Because we did not share her religious background, she dismissed all of our comments that anger is normal and does not mean possession by the devil. As an alternative course of action and with her permission, we discussed her situation with the minister that she had indicated she liked and greatly admired. Following consultation with us, the minister visited her in her home and told her essentially the same things we had been saying—that anger is normal and does not mean possession by the devil. She arrived at the next therapy session both greatly relieved and ready to work on more productive means of expressing her anger. (Dunckley et al., 1980, pp. 82-83)

Such contributions by ministers are, of course, in addition to the expanded role they might play as pastoral counselors (Vayhinger, 1980). A number of options involve rural congregations in providing services. These alternatives entail mobilizing an indigenous sense of commitment and good will that often exists within the membership. On the level of direct service, rural churches can develop and coordinate a volunteer transportation service that would involve parishioners in offering their services to take elderly people to the doctor or on shopping trips. Such transportation services, often based on the informal exchange of rides for cash, a cake, or preserves the recipient "put up" the previous year, already exist in Colton and in many rural areas.

There is also great potential for activating rural congregations to provide social support and reassurance for elderly parishioners. One noteworthy venture is the lay ministry to elderly and shut-in members of the Rural Valley United Presbyterian Church developed by the Reverend John Stevenson using seven volunteers from his western Pennsylvania congregation (Stevenson, 1980). This project involved a four session training program during which the volunteers were instructed in the theological basis of the proposed lay ministry, were provided with basic information on gerontology and were involved in discussions of listening skills, communicating and the value of reminiscing and life review in elderly people's lives. The volunteers were then asked to make visits to elderly parishioners each month as part of their ministry.

Involving parishioners in ministry with the elderly provides a useful initiative in moving toward a final option that is increasingly coming into vogue in urban areas—developing support groups for older people or their families (Aronson, Levin and Lipkowitz, 1984). There are several problems associated with transferring such approaches to rural areas. First, with regard to support groups for problems such as Alzheimer's disease, there is the difficulty occasioned by the absence of individuals with professional training qualified to lead such groups. Second, individuals in rural areas tend to be extremely reluctant to be identified as needing support. One solution to this problem may lie in expanding of the traditional role of the church congregation as a support group for its elderly members and their families (Tilberg, 1984, p. 62). Panel discussions and lecture series at churches focused on themes such as "You and Your Aging Parent" and "Intergenerational Relations and the Elderly" are becoming increasingly common as the aging of congregations becomes more apparent.

Enhancing Indigenous Support Networks

A third area in which rural churches may provide support to elderly parishioners builds upon the knowledge which conscientious ministers rapidly develop of the "society of the old" that exists as a distinctive sub-culture within most rural communities (Rowles, 1980).

Many ministers, as a result of pastoral visits, are acutely aware of the localized clusters of mutually supportive elderly people and their younger neighbors described earlier. They are cognizant of the telephone networks that activate to spread the latest news and gossip. A critical contribution can be made as a result of the respect, trust, and moral authority with which ministers are imbued. This contribution involves carefully considered efforts to integrate older people who seem to be "outsiders" within the supportive network provided by local clusters. However, cautions are in order. Some old people have been "loners" throughout their lives. They may be resentful of an intrusion, however benignly intended. In most rural communities there are also individuals, sometimes as a result of longstanding animosities, who simply do not get along. While forcing them to interact may appeal to a sense of the need for reconciliation, it may also disrupt an otherwise smoothly functioning support cluster.

Enhancing indigenous support networks is also possible through activating hitherto underused segments of a congregation. The youth of the church might be organized into a resource pool to undertake simple chores such as collecting groceries or cutting the grass for elderly parishioners. The benefits of such programs are often mutual. A second option is establishing a "chore team" comprised of men within the church, especially those who have recently retired who possess skills and experience that can be put to use in the service of the elderly (Tilberg, 1984, p. 67). In return for the cost of materials and perhaps a home baked pie this chore team can undertake minor and, on occasion, major repair jobs.

Providing Educational Programs

In recent years many churches have expanded their religious education role to include educational endeavors in the secular domain. Such efforts are especially appropriate in rural areas. Church facilities are often excellent sites for workshops or panel discussions. Moreover, rural ministers are often among the more educated members of the community and frequently have access to educational resources. Third, in many rural areas the church is viewed by parishioners as a focus of innovation. Finally, as Stevenson (1980) has noted, churches have a moral responsibility to engage in activities that enhance a sense of "mystical communion" among parishioners and are consonant with the ideal of the church as a servant of God. The growing popularity of church sponsored colloquia on intergenerational relationships and on caring for aged parents has already been noted. Such efforts serve an important consciousness raising role. Other more intensive options are also worthy of consideration. One alternative currently being implemented in West Virginia under the aegis of a Robert Wood Johnson Foundation grant, involves the use of church facilities for a four week seminar for congregations wishing to learn more about gerontology. The anticipation is that bringing together rural congregations within this context will not only increase awareness of aging issues but will also enhance the role of congregations as informal support groups for the vulnerable.

In order to establish viable educational programs it is critical that ministers improve their own understanding of aging and the aged (Karcher and Karcher, 1980). Some seminaries have begun to introduce gerontological content within their curricula (Tilberg, 1984). Most universities and community colleges now offer courses in gerontology that are open to individuals who are not full-time students. Not only do such programs facilitate increased understanding of the elderly but also they provide a means by which contact can be made with professionals who are characteristically willing to make their expertise available within church sponsored educational programs.

As increasing understanding and appreciation of the needs and resources of the elderly begins to become a part of the "religious ambience" of rural communities, it may be possible to break down psychological barriers that discourage the elderly from participating in church sponsored educational programs to address their special needs. We may envisage a time when presentations on the dietary needs of the elderly or on podiatry and aging might become a routinely accepted component of the mission of the rural church.

SPECIAL CONSIDERATIONS IN DEVELOPING CHURCH SPONSORED PROGRAMS FOR THE RURAL AGED

So far, a potpourri of strategies has been presented. Some have already been implemented by individual churches. Others are relatively simple alternatives that can be developed at minimal cost. Clearly, each congregation will select from the array of possibilities according to local circumstances. Regardless of the path to be followed, several considerations are essential to ensuring even a modicum of success.

It is vital to incorporate the elderly in the process of developing rural ministries. Such involvement means more than token representation on committees. It entails using the elderly's intimate knowledge of the local "society of the old" as a basis for developing a community specific strategy. Involvement also entails acknowledging and legitimating skills that older parishioners characteristically conceal with protestations of inadequacy such as, "I'm not really qualified to do that." The authority and trust with which the clergy are held can be a critical asset in instilling confidence. Particularly important is the need to embrace older people with skills, experience, and vigor, who are in their immediately post retirement years. Special efforts should be made to involve elderly men who traditionally have tended to avoid high levels of church involvement and yet have so much to offer.

At the same time, it is important to ensure that efforts to involve the elderly in rural ministries do not conflict with existing contributions they may be making. In Colton, Bill, a retired railroad engineer, in the several years before his death, was known as an individual who would provide rides to the doctor to the elderly ladies in the community. He would formally accept no payment for this service. However, it had become common practice for recipients upon leaving his car to leave a couple of dollars, or a loaf of zucchini bread on the seat. While Bill was alive, it would have been inappropriate for the church to develop its own volunteer transportation service.

This illustration implies the need for careful planning of rural ministries to the elderly (Kerr, 1980). First, there is a need to mobilize the indigenous sense of commitment and concern that pervades most congregations. The next logical step would be an assessment of the specific needs of the local elderly population and the resources available to the church. Once this has been accomplished it is possible to develop church based strategies that are consonant with local conditions.

Rural society in most regions of the United States is undergoing rapid change. Part of the change is generational, as elderly populations accustomed to what Mead termed a "postfigurative" culture, characterized by low mobility, minimal social change, and adherence to a parental role model for successive generations, gradually give way to a more cosmopolitan mobile rural society in which such traditions are abandoned (Mead, 1970). A second component of change stems from the evolving demography of rural areas. It is becoming increasingly necessary to reconcile the needs of older people who throughout their lives have been immersed in the mores of rural culture with a generation of newcomers with very different needs, expectations and resources. In future years, as the newcomers become more frail, it is they who may have the greatest need for support from the church community.

It is fitting to close by returning to Audrey. As she stands wistfully by her window watching her neighbors travel to church, she expresses no resentment that she cannot be with them. Though her frailty is such that now she could not attend the service even if all the physical barriers that first stopped her from making the trip were removed, her church is still the fulcrum of her life. She knows she is still part of a caring congregation. Her situation reflects perhaps the most important gift to its elderly parishioners that can be bestowed by the rural church, a transcendent sense of caring and concern for the personhood of the individual.

NOTES

1. In order to protect the confidentiality of participants in the project from which some of the illustrations in this paper are drawn, all proper names are pseudonyms.

2. The term minister is used generically to indicate a member of the clergy from any denomination and subsumes priests, rabbis, reverends, pastors and other comparable representatives of formal religious organizations.

REFERENCES

Aday, R.H., and Miles, L.A., "Long Term Impacts of Rural Migration of the Elderly: Implications for Research," *The Gerontologist, 22,* 1982, pp. 331-336.

Aronson, M.K., Levin, G., and Lipkowitz, R., "A Community-Based Family/Patient

Group Program For Alzheimer's Disease," *The Gerontologist, 24,* 1984, pp. 339-342.

Atchley, R.C., and Miller, S.J., "Housing and Households of the Rural Aged." In T.O. Byerts, S.C. Howell and L.A. Pastalan (Eds.) *Environmental Context of Aging: Lifestyles, Environmental Quality and Living Arrangements* New York: Garland STPM Press, 1979, pp. 62-79.

Beall, G.T., Thompson, M.M., Godwin, F., and Donahue, W.T., *Housing Older Persons in Rural America: A Handbook on Congregate Housing* Washington, D.C.: International Center for Social Gerontology, 1981.

Blazer, D., and Palmore, E., "Religion and Aging on A Longitudinal Panel," *The Gerontologist 16,* 1976, pp. 82-85.

Bornstein, M.H., "The Pace of Life: Revisited," *International Journal of Psychology 14,* 1979, pp. 83-90.

Bylund, R.A., Crawford, C.O., and LeRay, N.L., "Housing Quality of the Elderly: A Rural-Urban Comparison," *Journal of Minority Aging 4,* 1979, pp. 14-24.

Collier, C.M., A Community Study of Aging and Religion Among Rural Pennsylvania Germans. Unpublished Ph.D. Dissertation, University of Massachusetts, 1978.

Coward, R.T., "Planning Community Services for the Rural Elderly: Implications from Research" *The Gerontologist, 19,* 1979 p. 275-282.

Coward, R.T., and Kerckhoff, R.K., *The Rural Elderly: Program Planning Guidelines* Ames, Iowa, North Central Regional Center for Rural Development, Iowa State University, 1978.

Coward, R.T., and Lee, G.R., *The Elderly in Rural Society: Every Fourth Elder* New York: Springer, 1984.

Donnenwerth, G.V., Guy, R., and Norvell, M.J., "Life Satisfaction Among Older Persons: Rural-Urban and Racial Comparisons," *Social Service Quarterly 59,* 1978, pp. 578-583.

Dunckley, R.A., Lutes, C.J., Wooten, J.N., and Kooken, R.A., "Therapy Approaches With Rural Elders." In S.S. Sargent (Ed.) *Nontraditional Therapy and Counseling With the Aging.* New York: Springer Publishing Co., 1980, pp. 74-99.

Ergood, B., and Shelley, R.K., "Correlates of Life Satisfaction in a Rural Elderly Population." Paper presented at Annual Meeting of North Central Sociological Association, 1979.

Flemming, A.S., "The Role of the Church as Educator and Advocate in Aging Issues." Paper presented at National Symposium on the Church and Aging, Zion, Illinois, September 25, 1984.

Fuguitt, G.V., and Tordella, S.J., "Elderly Net Migration: The New Trend of Nonmetropolitan Population Change," *Research on Aging, 2,* 1980, pp. 191-204.

Glover, E.E., "Nutrition and the Rural Elderly." In P.K.H. Kim and C.P. Wilson, (Eds.) *Toward Mental Health of the Rural Elderly* Washington, D.C.: University Press of America, 1981, pp. 97-116.

Grams, A., and Fengler, A.P., "Vermont Elders: No Sense of Deprivation," *Perspective on Aging 10,* 1981, pp. 12-15.

Hynson, L.M., "Rural-Urban Differences in Satisfaction Among the Elderly," *Rural Sociology 40,* 1976, pp. 269-275.

Karcher, C.J., and Karcher, B.C., "Higher Education and Religion: Potential Partners in Service to the Rural Elderly," *Educational Gerontology 5,* 1980, pp. 409-421.

Kerr, H.L., *How to Minister to Senior Adults in Your Church* Nashville, TN: Broadman Press, 1980.

Kivett, V.R., "Discriminators of Loneliness Among the Rural Elderly: Implications for Intervention." *The Gerontologist 19,* 1979, pp. 108-115.

Konan, M., Tweed, D. and Longest, J., "Poverty and the Distribution of Mental Health Resources: Rural-Urban Comparisons," *Rural America 4* 1979, pp. 283-284.

Lee, G.R., and Lassey, M.L. "Rural-Urban Differences Among the Elderly: Economic, Social and Subjective Factors," *Journal of Social Issues 36,* 1980, pp. 62-74.

Lozier, J., and Althouse, R., "Social Enforcement of Behavior Toward Elders in an Appalachian Mountain Settlement," *The Gerontologist 14,* 1974, pp. 69-80.

Lucore, S., Lutheran Services of Lehigh Valley, Inc., Personal Communication. October 28, 1984.

McCoy, J.L., and Brown, D.L., "Health Status Among Low Income Elderly Persons: Rural-Urban Differences," *Social Security Bulletin, 41,* 1978, pp. 14-16.

McKelvey, D.J., "Transportation Issues and Problems of the Rural Elderly," In S.M. Golant (Ed.) *Location and Environment of Elderly Population* Washington, D.C.: V.H. Winston, 1979, pp. 135-140.

Mead, M., *Culture and Commitment: A Study of the Generation Gap* Garden City, New York: Natural History Press, Doubleday, 1970.

Nelson, G., "Social Services to the Urban and Rural Aged: The Experience of Area Agencies on Aging," *The Gerontologist, 20* 1980, pp. 200-207.

Ortega, S.T., Crutchfield, R.D., and Rushing, W.A., "Race Differences in Elderly Personal Wellbeing: Friendship, Family and Church," *Research on Aging 5,* 1983, pp. 101-118.

Patton, C.V., "Age Groupings and Travel in a Rural Area," *Rural Sociology 40,* 1975, pp. 55-63.

Pihlblad, C.T., "Culture, Life Style and Social Environment of the Small Town," In R.C. Atchley and T.O. Byerts (Eds.) *Rural Environments and Aging* Washington, D.C.: Gerontological Society, 1975, pp. 47-62.

Pihlblad, C.T., and McNamara, R.L., "Social Adjustments of Elderly People In Three Small Towns," In A.M. Rose and W.A. Peterson (Eds.) *Older People and Their Social World* Philadelphia: Davis, 1965, pp. 49-73.

Powers, E.A., Keith, P., and Goudy, W.J., "Family Relationships and Friendships Among the Rural Aged." In T.O. Byerts, S.C. Howell and L.A. Pastalan (Eds.) *Environmental Context of Aging: Lifestyles, Environmental Quality and Living Arrangements* New York: Garland STPM Press, 1979, pp. 80-101.

Rowles, G.D., "Growing Old 'Inside': Aging and Attachment to Place in an Appalachian Community." In N. Datan and N. Lohmann (Eds.) *Transitions of Aging* New York: Academic Press, 1980, pp. 153-170.

Rowles, G.D. "The Surveillance Zone as Meaningful Space For the Aged," *The Gerontologist 21,* 1981, pp. 304-311.

Rowles, G.D. "Geographical Dimensions of Social Support in Rural Appalachia." In G.D. Rowles and R.J. Ohta (Eds.) *Aging and Milieu: Environmental Perspectives on Growing Old* New York: Academic Press, 1983a, pp. 111-130.

Rowles, G.D. "Between Worlds: A Relocation Dilemma for the Appalachian Elderly," *International Journal of Aging and Human Development 17,* 1983b, pp. 301-314.

Rowles, G.D., "Place and Personal Identity in Old Age: Observations From Appalachia," *Journal of Environmental Psychology 3,* 1983c, pp. 219-313.

Rowles, G.D., "Aging in Rural Environments." In I. Altman, J. Wohlwill, and M.P. Lawton (Eds.) *Human Behavior and Environment: The Elderly and the Physical Environment* New York: Plenum Press, 1984, pp. 129-152.

Stevenson, J.R., The Development of a Lay Ministry to Elderly and Shut-in Members of the Rural Valley United Presbyterian Church. Doctor of Ministry Dissertation, Drew University, New Jersey, 1980.

Stojanovic, D.J., "The Dissemination of Information About Medicare to Low-Income Rural Residents," *Rural Sociology 37,* 1972, pp. 253-260.

Taietz, P., and Milton, S., "Rural-Urban Differences in Structure of Services for the Elderly in Upstate New York Counties," *Journal of Gerontology 34,* 1979, pp. 429-437.

Tilberg, C.W., *Revolution Underway: An Aging Church in an Aging Society* Philadelphia: Fortress Press, 1984.

United States Bureau of the Census.

Vayhinger, J.M., "The Approach of Pastoral Psychology." In S.S. Sargent (Ed.) *Nontraditional Therapy and Counseling With the Aging* New York: Springer Publishing Co., 1980, pp. 74-99.

Examining the Role of the Church in the Aging Network

Rev. James W. Ellor, D.Min, A.M., C.S.W., A.C.S.W.
Robert B. Coates, Ph.D.

ABSTRACT. Although churches are invaluable resources, few studies have investigated the total range of services available with emphasis on how these ministries interact with the local aging network. To better understand the role of the church in the aging network, a four year action research project was developed. Six communities were studied in depth: interviews were conducted with clergy, social service agency directors, and seniors; community models for working towards common ministry goals were developed; and curricular materials for seminaries were generated based on research results. This paper presents some of the significant findings of this research project, including the various groups of seniors found in the local congregation and the programs and services which exist in local churches. Study implications are discussed in relation to the current role of the church's work in aging; methods of coordinating services both among churches and between churches and local service agencies; the training of clergy to work with the elderly; and the role of the national church.

Since the time of the apostles, older people have related to their local congregations. This relationship has gone without question for centuries. However, with the increase in life expectancy and the growing numbers of seniors in our congregations, has come a change in the makeup of many of our local churches. In the last forty years the scales have begun to tip from churches whose memberships reflect large numbers of children and a smaller numbers of seniors, to churches, particularly the smaller, mainline churches, which have equal or greater numbers of seniors in the congregations.

Rev. James W. Ellor is a member of the faculty, National College of Education, 2S361 Glen Park Road, Lombard, Illinois 60148, and Parish Associate, Lumen Christi United Presbyterian Church, Naperville, Illinois 60540. Robert B. Coates is Director of Research, Pact Institute of Justice, Valparaiso, Indiana 46383.

This project was funded by The Retirement Research Foundation.

While some congregations have not begun to feel this shift, those that have need to consider the implications of this demographic shift on programming and policy.

In this paper we will begin by relating information on the demographics of churches represented in this research. We will then identify the various ways churches provide for the needs of the elderly and how these efforts are reflected in the ''Aging Network.'' Next, we will discuss the implications for the training needs of seminarians to work with the elderly, and conclude with a discussion of the implications for denominational policy makers.

THE ELDERLY IN THE LOCAL CONGREGATION

Numerous authors have discussed the importance of religion in the lives of the elderly. Possibly the most important statistic for a discussion of programs in churches that has been generated by these writers is suggested by Harris et al. (Harris et al., 1975, pp. 180-181) who suggest that 71% of persons aged 65 or over felt religion was very important in their lives. This same poll noted that 79% of the seniors surveyed had attended church or synagogue within the past two weeks. Seniors attend church more regularly and give a larger percentage of their income than any other age group. Examination of the demographic statistics in the churches of the six communities studied during this research project found that the average church in this ecumenical sample reported ten percent more seniors than is reflected in the percentage of elderly in the community. Thus if the percentage of seniors in the community was equal to the national average, a community with 11% of its population over the age of sixty five, would reflect 21% of the membership of the local churches and synagogues (Tobin & Ellor, 1983).

In a second study of the alumni of a specific seminary, the authors further refined this data by controlling for staff size. Among this national sample of predominately United Church of Christ clergy, the average church reported 31% of its members over the age of sixty five. However, when we compare congregations with a single ordained minister with those who have more than one, solo pastors average 266 total members, who have an average income of $22,313 and reflect 34% of their membership over the age of 65. By contrast, the multiple staff church averaged 775 members, where income averaged $27,572 and they have only 25% persons over the age of sixty five. Thus the congregations with the lower per person income, smaller congregational size, and fewer clergy have the higher percentage of seniors in the congregation (Ellor & Coates, 1984).

These trends seemed to be consistent in all six communities, which included neighborhoods within a large city, as well as suburban communities. The exceptions were the congregation that was in a suburb that was established after 1955, churches that had been established within the past ten years and large "fundamentalist" often non-denominational Bible churches. These congregations had lower percentages of seniors and often reported that the seniors that were members were younger and in need of fewer services. It should be noted that our samples are predominantly made up of white churches. We cannot suggest from our data that they will reflect churches in Black, Hispanic, or communities made up of persons from other minority groups.

When we examine the various groups of seniors within the congregation, we encounter the expected variety of individual people, with individual needs. If we categorize these persons, our study found that there are four groups. Three groups commonly discussed in the literature are the well elderly and shut-ins or the frail elderly and the families of the elderly. Our studies identified a third group that we call the "service shut-in." The well elderly are often those persons that Neugarten calls the "young old" (Neugarten, 1974). These persons are sometimes referred to as middle aged persons who have passed their sixty-fifth birthday. They are physically well and their needs have not changed significantly over the past ten to fifteen years. By contrast the shut-in is a senior that is unable to leave home due to physical or emotional illness. Shanas et al. suggest that eight percent of all seniors are homebound and three percent of this group are bedbound at any given time (Shanas et al., 1968). Many churches place such persons on pastoral calling lists.

While the groups of well elderly and shut-ins are familiar to most congregations, our study identified a third group that we called "service shut-ins." These seniors are more difficult to identify. They are not severely physically disabled, but are homebound for other reasons. It is important to note that one of the reasons that this group is so difficult to identify, is that when they do attend church, they appear to be physically well and respond to any inquiry as to their well being with the suggestion that "everything is fine." However, upon investigation, they may be quite lonely and feel as though they are becoming detached from the church. Some are homebound simply because they are unable to drive. Some are homebound because, while they do drive, they only do so when the weather is good and their car is in proper working condition. Still others may be homebound only in winter, but are able to get out during the other seasons of the year. In some communities they may be homebound due to loss of income which has left them without adequate clothes or money to socialize. Finally, some may be unable to leave home for emotional reasons. For example, the unresolved grief of losing a spouse may render an otherwise healthy senior homebound. In each of these cases, if the church provides such services as transportation or counseling, these seniors are generally able to return to active participation in congregational life. When these services are not available, this study observed that many seniors in this group were quite bitter. As they were not recognized as homebound, they were not visited, yet they felt that they were unable to fully participate in the activities offered by their church.

The final group of persons that need to be recognized when ministering with seniors are the families of the elderly. Particularly when they are the caretakers of the senior, a spouse or even a daughter can become every bit as homebound as the senior if the senior can not be left alone. Increasing numbers of caretakers of the elderly are in fact elderly themselves, either spouses, or even children. When this is the case, additional concerns of these seniors will need to be addressed. Unfortunately, this group is often overlooked in ministry.

THE NATURE OF PROGRAMS
AND SERVICES IN CHURCHES

In our investigation into the role of the church in the aging network, we have found that the services provided by churches fall into four basic groups. These are:

1. Religious Programs
2. Pastoral Care Programs
3. The Church As Host
4. The Church As Service Provider

In the language of the social sciences, these services range from informal to formal. Some of them involve trained professionals, both clergy and others, and some do not. Indeed, many of the people doing the actual work in these programs were not clergy. While we made no effort to obtain information as to the quality or effectiveness of these programs and services, it is clear that this varies from group to group and service to service.

Religious Programs

The category of religious programs includes the sort of activities that one would most likely anticipate emanating from the church or synagogue. For example, this includes the weekend worship services that are held in a majority of churches. In an effort to provide an example of the programs available in church I will use the example of one of the six communities in our study. Elm Town is part of the first ring of suburbs which surrounds a major midwestern city. A population of approximately 55,000 persons is supported in a land space of 4.6 square miles. Elm Town is considered by many to be an older community. Both its buildings, and more importantly, its people are growing old, with 16.5% of the population over the age of 65. Elm Town has 48 churches and one synagogue. It is a service rich community with over eighteen services identified as primarily providing for the needs of the elderly.

When we examine the religious programs available in Elm Town, we find that 76% of the churches have Bible studies, 38% hold special worship services for seniors and 71% participate in a local holiday food basket distribution. Also of concern in this category of programs are the various activities that churches engage in that are intended to aid seniors in participating in worship. In Elm Town 100% of the clergy stated that they provide some sort of transportation assistance for helping seniors to participate in church activities. The clergy also noted that 88% of their congregations have public address systems at least in their sanctuary and another 15% had hearing aids for use during worship. While many of the churches in this community still have architectural barriers, 76% of the churches noted that they would be able to assist seniors up the stairs.

The pastoral care literature reminds us that unlike other activities and groups, the church is generally a part of the individual's life from cradle to grave. The church baptizes, marries, and buries, with everything in between. For many seniors the church offers a continuity in their lives, that may not otherwise be available outside of the family. It is often the religious activities that are continued after other activities have ceased.

Pastoral Care Programs

The next group refers to the pastoral care programs available in the church. This category breaks into two sub-groups, services for individuals, and programs for groups. These programs and services range from the informal to the formal. They are generally directed toward the members of the congregation and are a part of the general life of the congregation. The services for individuals in Elm Town include visitation to seniors in the hospital (100%), visitation to the homebound (94%), visitation to nursing homes (88%), telephone reassurance (71%), home delivered meals (33%), and assistance with housekeeping (32%). It can also include such things as general transportation (62%), food distribution programs (62%), and free clothing (35%). As a general rule, it should be noted that when the clergy reported that they do these things they are not implying that they keep a large store of food available, or that they run a dial-a-bus transportation program. Rather, if Mrs. Jones calls the pastor in need of a ride, the pastor calls Mrs. Smith, who takes Mrs. Jones to the doctor. If Mrs. Jones is having trouble preparing meals, the pastor may call on the ladies club to help her out. Were the pastor to receive more than a handful of such requests in any given month, they would not be able to handle them.

When we are discussing the individual services, we can see that in this category, the church acts in much the same way as a friend, or neighbor. Froland et al. (Froland et al., 1981) have suggested that the role of the church in the human service network is as a natural helping neighbor. As one pastor stated "Our church helps its members because they are a part of our family, not because we see ourselves as social service agencies." (King, 1982)

The second subgroup of pastoral care programs are the group activities. In Elm Town these may include senior clubs or groups (74%), educational discussion groups (74%), and discussion groups for younger people on aging (24%). In other communities this has included support groups for adult children dealing with aging parents and other self help groups for seniors. (e.g., stroke and diabetes clubs, etc.). The focus of these group activities may, or may not, include what could be called religious concerns. While some advertising may be done to attract participants from the community, they generally do not involve a fee and may not even include a leader specifically trained to perform this type of service. These group activities move the church one step closer to the type of service provided by social agencies. However, they are still not considered as such by either the church, or the participants.

In summary, the pastoral care programs and services range in approach from informal neighbor helping neighbor activities, to more formal types of counseling and group activities. It should be noted that the term pastoral in this context does not mean that the professional clergy are the only ones involved. Often these services and programs are developed and led by lay members of the congregation. While clergy are often interested and supportive of such activities, Steinitz (Steinitz, 1981) found that a majority of services developed by churches are led by lay persons, not clergy. Sometimes these lay church members hold professional social work or counseling degrees, but often this is not the case. They are people who are concerned and want to help. Indeed, Ellor et al. (Ellor et al., 1983) note that a lack of lay leadership is often the primary barrier to the church's ability to provide services to the elderly. Thus, pastoral care programs are generally seen by both the church and the participants as emanating out of the congregation as a part of their care and concern for the members of their community. They are not intended to be formal social service programs.

The Church as Host

Particularly since the 1972 Amendments to the Older Americans Act, the Church has become host to numerous social service activities. Possibly the most common of these are the meal programs. It is not unusual to find the local Area Agency on Aging providing some of their lunch programs in the basement of a local church or synagogue. In recent years, churches have become conscious of the fact that their education buildings stand empty during the week seeing their greatest use only on weekends. In Elm Town we found two instances of the church loaning or renting space to local social agencies. This includes a nutrition site and a home companion service. It is important to note that with this category of services, there may or may not be significant interaction between the worshiping congregation and the consumers of the social service. In effect, the agency is borrowing the church building, but not the congregation. Even though the service may be available to the members of the congregation we have received mixed reports. It has been reported to our researchers that at least in one case, it is easier to get the members of the church to volunteer to assist the program than it is to attract the members of the congregation who need the service into it. However, other cases were reported that reflect active involvement by the worshiping congregation.

The Church as Service Provider

In this final category, the local church actually creates a social service agency. Generally in response to a gap within the local social service network, the church will create services for one of two reasons. Either the need for the service has become clear and the church is in a position to respond, or the service may exist elsewhere in the community, but the other service may adhere to a value system that is contrary to that of the church.

In Elm Town, one example reflects the church as a service provider. One of the local Catholic churches, with some assistance from other churches, created a home companion service, because at the time it was unavailable. This service has been available for over ten years and is now publicly funded. While housed in the original Catholic Church, it is a formal social service agency. In other communities churches have created housing projects for the elderly, as well as other types of social services. Examples of churches providing services that adhere to their values include nursing homes, retirement facilities, and senior centers. Possibly the oldest example of this type of endeavor is our parochial school system.

Please note that we are not including in this analysis the services, programs, and institutions created by denominational groups. While such things as Catholic Charities and Jewish Social Services are not unimportant to the local congregation, we are referring only to those services that are actually provided by one or more local congregations within a specific geographic community.

THE ROLE OF THE CHURCH
IN THE AGING NETWORK

As we examine the role of the church in the aging network, we can see that over time it has changed. While a majority of retirement facilities at the turn of the century were run by religious groups, today this is no longer true. Since the turn of the century the church has moved from providing a majority of human services, to a less formal form of service provision. While some churches today continue to provide formal social services, both as individual congregations and by supporting social service agencies associated with their denominations or communities, they tend to do so in a gap filling capacity, while allowing publicly funded agencies to provide a majority of the services. Indeed, in today's social service climate, when the church does work to create a formal human service or social service agency, it often seeks, after a brief period of time, to spin it off as an independent entity.

It is important to understand that while churches are valuable resources made up of people who care about the plight of others, most do not conceive of themselves as service providers. The church is primarily a caring community that cares about the well-being of its members, as well as those around them. It is out of this notion of being a caring community that social service activities emanate. Among the ramifications of this is the fact that often churches lack the technical expertise or financial support contained in the social service agency for the provision of the service. In short, they are often long on caring and short on expertise and money. It is equally important to note that since the church is a volunteer association, it often does not have a great deal of time available from its professional staff (e.g., the clergy) to direct the activities. Thus, as a source of service provision to people in need, many churches have a great deal of goodwill, but often lack technical expertise and adequate professional staff.

While it is difficult to capture in the survey format, the churches in our example, Elm Town, play a quiet role as a support system to the social service agencies. In at least one case it was a concerned pastor who promoted the creation, by the village, of a senior center. Churches also support local agencies through volunteer efforts. While these types of assistance are difficult to quantify, they are an important part of the churches understanding of its approach to assisting the local service network.

When we compare the community of Elm Town with the others in our study, we can see that it is exceptional in many ways. This community is quite involved in everything from Bible study to community concerns. It is also a community that is service rich. It has been the observation of our project that in communities where there is a great deal of human need and few social service agencies, the church plays a greater role in providing both formal and informal social services. Finally, unlike many other communities, Elm Town has a senior services coordinating council that includes one of the local clergy. While this pastor does not represent all of the churches and synagogues in the community, she or he is elected by the local clergy council and can give input on church concerns to the coordinating council.

Thus, when we examine the role of the church in the aging network of Elm Town, we can see that it does not play one role, but many roles. The church provides a caring community for its members. It also provides many informal services similar to those that one could request from one's family. In this community, churches provide group activities and concrete social services, by providing space in their buildings, through direct service, or by assisting the creation of social service agencies. However, its main role is as a helping neighbor. This would seem to be an appropriate role for them in this community, as it is rich in formal social service resources. However, in the current changing climate of budget cuts and reduction of services, it remains to be seen what changes will be made in Elm Town in the role of the church and synagogue.

COLLABORATION OF PROGRAMS

As we have suggested in the previous section, the programs and services provided by churches are clearly important to the elderly in each community. However, our studies found that actual collaboration between the local churches and social service agencies varied from church to church and community to community. A majority of churches provide religious programs, respond informally to concrete needs (such as for food and transportation), make some referrals to local social services and even, at times when an unmet need is identified, develop a formal program. Less frequently, however, do churches jointly sponsor programs with other churches or collaborate directly with social agencies. The most common examples of sharing with community agencies were in programs that provide volunteers to do friendly visiting and assist in local transportation, or programs that provide food or clothing during holiday periods. Far less common were examples of case consultation, or coordination of services.

Our project identified several methods employed by the churches that do work with other churches. Albeit, not as frequently utilized as might be desirable, these approaches include referral of persons in need, attendance at meetings of service providers, development of mutual workshops or inservices as well as specific efforts to develop joint programs. While some specific clergy were active in local agencies as board members and advocates for seniors, some agencies were even started by clergy or specific churches, a majority of churches seemed to seek to spin off any social agency that might have been created by its membership. Ongoing activities that slowly begin to resemble that of social service agencies, begin to be taken over by social work professionals and eventually, often as a result of federal funding, become independent agencies.

ENHANCING NETWORKING BETWEEN CHURCHES AND SOCIAL SERVICE AGENCIES

As we look at the various networking efforts, our project has found that the temptation of many agencies and individuals attempting to organize networks is to set the goal of complete collaboration. However, we have found that collaboration is not an end in itself, but rather only one step along a continuum of possible relationships. These relationships range from communication to confederation. We have identified the elements of this continuum as follows:

—Communication: Verbal, written or other forms of communication between two or more organizations. Limited to sharing information or ideas between groups. This would include consultation.
—Cooperation: Two or more separate organizations plan and implement independent programs, but work toward similar, nonconflicting goals. The organizations share information but act on it independently. Organizations advertise for each other and try to avoid unnecessary duplication of services.
—Coordination: Two or more separate organizations work together as they plan and implement separate programs. Efforts are made to ensure the programs interact smoothly and avoid conflict, waste or unnecessary duplication of services. Organizations share information, advertise for each other and make referrals to each other.

—Collaboration: Two or more separate organizations join together to provide a single program or service. Each organization maintains its own identity, but resources are jointly shared.

—Confederation: Two or more organizations merge to provide programs or services. None of the participating organizations maintains a separate identity or separate resources (Ellor, 1983).

When setting the goals of any given effort, the organizing group must recognize that if they set their goals too high, they may be setting unrealistic expectations. If they are working in a community where communication seems to be limited, they will need to investigate to better understand the various problems. Such things as competition or negative past experiences will have a bearing on current relationships. While the actual reasons will vary, if they were anxiety producing to the various actors, it may be that the goal of communication is more realistic. Simply reestablishing conversation can be a major breakthrough. In other communities where the various agencies already work well together, the more complex goals of collaboration, or even confederation, may indeed be realistic.

Our project has found that there are three essential steps that need to be added to the characteristics of a team when applied to community networking. The first is, get to know your community. Whether this is done systematically through some sort of research instrument, or less formally through some sort of telephone, or person to person contact, the organizing group must get to know their community and understand the issues of the entire group of service providers. Too often we assume that because we have worked in a community for a period of years, we know what all of the issues are of that community. What we found in our surveys of the communities is that there were some unexpected opinions and perceptions of the community, that even people from the older established agencies were not always aware of. We have also found that as in working with a team, the more person to person contact, the better. This activity contains a secondary gain. It raises the expectation that something is going to happen. By going out to interview the appropriate people from the other agencies and groups, you will both communicate that their opinion is desired and that you are gathering this information for a purpose. This gives them some time to consider your project and whether or not they wish to be a part of it.

The second step is to select a neutral group, person, or agency, that will not be perceived by the other service providers as having a hidden agenda. In a couple of cases our project has observed that even an agency that wants to bring together the local network and has the personnel to do so, may not be perceived as being agenda free by the other agencies. If this organizing agency is felt to have hidden agendas, for example, to subsume the other agencies, or to get them to take over services that they can no longer afford due to budget cuts, they will frighten the other groups and agencies away and thus reduce the effectiveness of the network. Our project has found that it isn't always easy to find such an agency. However, if one includes a question in the initial investigation as to who would be appropriate to bring the groups together, they will generally tell you and assist with this issue.

Lastly we have found that the network initially needs to be organized around perceived needs. The agencies and groups must perceive a need to get together. If they don't, they won't. For example our project worked in one community where the agencies initially met around the needs of the elderly. However, it became increasingly clear that even the agencies that serve only seniors were at least as concerned about the local unemployment problem, that is quite high as were the family oriented services. Even though our project sees itself as advocates for the elderly, in this community the principles of good community organization would suggest that we should have switched to the issues and concerns around unemployment. We suspect that greater success will be obtained on our issues when we returned to the needs of the elderly once the focal needs of the unemployed were met.

Our work in six communities has suggested that one of the harder issues in networking is related to the inclusion of the informal caretakers. This is the group that is emerging in the literature under the title of Natural Helping Neighbors. Included in this group are: one's next door neighbor, friends, and other significant figures in the lives of the seniors. This body of literature has also suggested that such groups as churches, synagogues, and senior centers, are a part of this group, yet were often overlooked by the more formal medical and social service agencies when discussions of who to include in the network of services were entertained.

Often the greatest problem that had to be overcome, particularly when discussing the role of church and synagogue, is a lack of understanding of how they fit into the human service network. Informal helpers are often difficult to access from the perspective of the formal agency. While the senior may tell his or her physician that they have a friend that will come over to help out, it tends to leave such questions as, "Is the friend reliable?" and "Do they really know what is needed?" Beyond these issues, what if you have another neighbor that needs help? Will the samaritan be willing to lend assistance to both? These are questions that one wouldn't necessarily ask of a formal medical, or social service agency, but are most appropriate for the informal helper.

EDUCATION AND TRAINING NEEDS

In an effort to understand the educational and training needs of the elderly, a questionnaire was developed and mailed to the 157 alumni of one midwestern seminary that is associated with the United Church of Christ. The sample was composed of all of the persons that graduated within the past 25 years and who stated that they intended to enter the parish ministry. Seventy four questionnaires were returned from these clergy. Among the issues addressed in this survey were questions about the skills needed to minister with the aged. The respondents were asked to respond to a long list of possible skills to determine which ones they felt were the most important, thus noting which they felt to be important to be taught in seminary. Preaching and empathy are the most frequently used skills, with leading small groups, program evaluation, and visiting the homebound as skills also frequently relied upon. By contrast, psychological assessment, long term counseling, social policy analysis, analysis of individual social networks and family therapy skills are not used nearly as often. These latter skills areas typically receive low scores in terms of respondents feeling well prepared to use them. Thus it seems evident that respondents are doing what they feel best prepared to do. It is to clergy that these skills adequately meet the needs of the elderly and their families. One would expect that skills related to referral, social network analysis and family therapy or counseling should be quite relevant.

Working with a small sample does not always produce statistical trends of major significance. However, one trend that was derived from cross tabulation involved the number of persons on staff at the church. As noted above when we compare churches with a single pastor to those with a multiple staff, the congregation size of churches with solo pastors has 66% fewer members, 9% more elderly members, and their members have over five thousand dollars less per household to live on. When we compare this with the skills needed to work with the elderly, the solo pastor is somewhat more comfortable with empathy, counseling, assessment, small groups analysis of social networks, analysis of social policy, visitation of homebound, and crisis intervention. While clergy who are a part of multiple staff churches are at least somewhat more comfortable with referral, advocacy, program evaluation, community needs assessment, family therapy, and conflict resolution. This is an important finding as when similar analysis was done for such variables as congregation size, percentage of older members, training, age or sex of the respondent, there was little difference. These data reinforce the concept that the pastor who works for a multiple staff church has a very different picture of the aged. Multiple staff churches can afford to specialize in their ministry in areas such as work with the aged. However, the pastor who is the only ordained person on staff needs to be more of the Jack of All Trades.

While solo pastors work with more elderly persons, they generally can't afford to hire even a semi-retired pastor to help with visitation. If these data are consistent with the experience of other seminaries, the implications for education are that 71% of the graduates will be going to solo parishes, therefore needing to be trained as a Jack of All Trades. The skill of the generalist is in their ability to gain a few basic skills that can be used in a wide variety of situations. The generalist is less likely to specialize in work with part of the congregation, because there isn't another clergyperson to support the remaining groups. If we can assume that the income of the congregants is reflected in the income of the congregation, the solo pastor also has less resources to work with to address the needs of the elderly. Some authors have suggested that clergy suffer from the same age biases as the rest of society. However, research has suggested that this is not true (Longino, 1976). Possibly the reason that clergy are less involved in ministry with the aged than their access to the elderly would imply has more to do with the realities of being the only pastor of a church, than it does with ageism.

Skills clearly needed to work with the aged for the pastor who is the only ordained person in a congregation include the less technical, one to one skill of counseling, empathy, and visitation. The complexities of negotiating the social systems, and advocating for large numbers of people's needs seem to be more comfortable for the persons in multiple staff churches, where more time can be spent attending community meetings, and becoming involved with social agencies. The data suggests that it is not a matter of multiple staff clergy not being empathic, and solo clergy not doing referrals. We would suggest that time and size of the need are important variables. The church with only one pastor has less staff time to be able to devote to problems of a single group like the elderly. Therefore if relatively large numbers of people present with a variety of needs, it will be harder for them to address it. Seminary education needs to be able to reflect his type of a congregation, as well as the larger, multiple staff church with more resources.

IMPLICATIONS FOR NATIONAL CHURCH POLICY

Brief examination of the data from this project would suggest nine different items that should be considered for national policy. First, more information is needed to truly understand the demographics, programmatic, and training needs for ministry with the elderly. The information gathered here may or may not be generalizable beyond the limits of the samples. We would suggest that money be made available through primary and secondary church sources to provide research into the changing demographics, as well as the programmatic and training needs of this type of ministry.

A second implication responds to the needs of the pastors who labor without benefit of other clergy in their parish. Our study suggested that these churches have some unique needs. With lower per member income, fewer members, and higher percentages of seniors, these churches are often found in cities, in changing neighborhoods, and in older communities. Responding to the needs of the "small" church is in fact a matter of reflecting the needs of three out of five Protestant churches.

Third, the church should encourage collaboration of efforts in ministry, both with other churches as well as with social service agencies. While not always feasible, where possible, collaboration at at least the level of communication can reduce cost and duplication of efforts to all of the parties involved, while enhancing services developed with the aged. This could be done through the agencies that fund programs as well as by providing training and consultation for local groups through organizations like Lutheran Social Services.

Encouraging training for laity would be a fourth implication. As a majority of programs are run and staffed by laity, emphasis should be placed upon providing training for them. This is particularly important in light of the value that we would hold up, that ministry should be provided *with* the aged, not *for* the aged. This may involve educating both young and old on the fact that the elderly, sometimes even the shut-in have an important place as ministers, not just as the recipients of ministry.

Sixth, congregations should be assisted to examine their buildings to ensure that they are barrier free. This may or may not include ramps and elevators, it may or may not include hearing aids and public address systems, not just in the sanctuary. This will also include making programs available during the day as well as in the evening. It may also include providing transportation to both worship and other church activities.

Seventh, clergy, seminaries, and churches need to be educated about the value of research. Too often the value of research techniques in the local congregation is discarded with the perception that numbers are cold and uncaring.

Eighth, churches should be encouraged to develop an initiative to identify the needs of the silent seniors in both the congregation and community. Persons who have stopped attending worship, or persons who may not be members, but are known by a member may not actively pursue assistance, yet, with some help from churches and social agencies, can be assisted to live a little longer in the community.

Finally, the ninth implication is that clergy need to be reminded that both formal *and* informal ministries are needed to meet the needs of the aged. This means that further research and training needs to take place on when ministry needs to become formalized and intentional and when it is appropriate for it to be left as an informal process. This will have implications for the "style" of practice, as well as the actual performance of ministry.

CONCLUSION

In conclusion, it is clear that the rising number of seniors in our worshiping congregations need to be listened to, understood, and provided opportunities to minister to each other, as well as participating in every aspect of the ministry of the church. We can see that the church does not play one role in the lives of seniors or in the aging network. Rather it plays many roles. It provides a caring community for its members. It also provides many informal services similar to those that one could request from a family. Some churches have also begun to provide formal services that fill gaps in the local network of services. In an effort to respond to the many roles of the church, clergy and laity need to be trained to be able to utilize the expanding body of literature in Gerontology, while keeping in mind the differences between churches with only one pastor versus the needs of the multiple staff church. The elderly are one of our most valuable resources. In order to respond to the needs of the current generation, as well as those to come, we need to continue to listen to their needs, listen to that which has been learned by or colleagues, and work together in the ministry of God's love.

REFERENCES

Ellor, James W., Anderson-Ray, Susan M., Tobin, Sheldon S. "The Role of the Church in Services to the Elderly." *Interdisciplinary Topics in Gerontology.* 1983, *17,* 119-131.

Ellor, James W. "Bridging Churches and Social Service Agencies: Value Conflicts and Program Potential." *Social Work and Christianity: An International Journal.* 1983, *10,* 21-39.

Froland, C., Pancoast, D.L., Chapman, N.J., and Kimboko, P.J. *Helping Networks and Human Services.* Beverly Hills: Sage Publications, 1981.

Harris, L. and Associates. *The Myth and Reality of Aging in America.* Washington D.C.: National Council on the Aging, Inc., 1975, 180-181.

King, Rev. Personal communication, May, 1982.

Longino, C.F. and Kitson, Gay C., "Parish Clergy and the Aged: Examining Stereotypes." *The Journal of Gerontology.* 1976, *31,* 340-345.

Neugarten, B.L. "Age Groups in American Society and the Rise of the Young Old." *Annals of the American Academy of Political and Social Science.* 1974, *415,* 189-198.

Shanas, H. and Associates. *Old People in Three Industrial Societies.* New York: Atherton Press, 1968.

Steinitz, L.Y. "The Local Church as Support for the Elderly." *Journal of Gerontological Social Work,* 1981, *4,* 43-53.

Tobin, S.S. and Ellor, J.W. *Year End Report.* Unpublished manuscript, University of Chicago, 1983.

The Third Quarter of Life: Implications for American Religious Institutions

D. Lydia Bronte, Ph.D.

ABSTRACT. The average life expectancy in America has increased dramatically since the turn of the century, and has been accompanied by a lengthened period of vigor in middle life. This increased vitality in the late and middle years of life has provoked the realization that a new definition of the mature years is desperately needed. Thus, a refocus away from the traditional, magical age of 65 to the period between 50 and 75 years of age—the "third quarter of life"—is useful for developing new policies and practices which increase productive potential and life satisfaction for persons in that age group. "Third quarter Americans" pose a special challenge to religious institutions. Churches are called to respond to this challenge by creating vehicles for the utilization of talents and the nurture of individual inner growth.

INCREASED LIFE EXPECTANCY AND VITALITY

One of the most remarkable achievements of the twentieth century in the United States has been the lengthening of average life expectancy by more than twenty-five years. In 1900, life expectancy at birth in this country was about 48 years. To be sure, there were a number of people who lived longer, but very few people reached advanced ages. Today, life expectancy at birth is around 75 and steadily rising. Serious scientific predictions indicate that the average life expectancy may rise to nearly one hundred years sometime in the twenty-first century.

Half of this accomplishment has come from a great reduction in the deaths of infants and children. Only about three-quarters of the

---

D. Lydia Bronte is Consultant and Staff Director, The Aging Society Project, Carnegie Corporation of New York, 437 Madison Avenue, New York, New York 10022.

117

babies born in 1900 could be expected to live to age 19. Now almost all children—98%—survive that long.

The remainder of the life expectancy increase comes from the postponement of adult death to older ages. In 1900, a group of 20 year olds subject to the prevailing death rates would face tough odds against living into old age: Only 53% of them would reach age 65, and a mere 18% would survive to age 80. By 1982, the rate of premature adult deaths had declined so drastically that 80% of the 20-year-olds would reach 65, and fully 45%—almost half of the group—would survive to 80.

Life expectancy in later life is still growing, and it has been accompanied by a lengthening of the period of vigor in middle life. This development contradicts in important ways the conventional image of the life course, especially with the interlocking concepts of "retirement" and old age. For fifty years the idea of retirement at age 65 has shaped our thinking about the upper boundaries of life. By 65 a person was old: he could no longer contribute to a fast-paced competitive society. I use the pronoun "he" advisedly since it was a male pattern of work and retirement that shaped the notions of old age for the entire society. In fact this pattern never applied to all adults, since it is based on a work history that until a few years ago was characteristic in our society only of men. Women have had a very different sequence of work experience—one in which there was little paid work and no real cessation of work in the mature years, though the intensity and focus of their jobs as "homemakers" changed with the departure of their grown children from the household.

These variations notwithstanding, the retirement-at-age-65 model was stimulated by the widespread difficulty experienced by men over 60 in finding work during the Great Depression. It was formalized in 1935 by the passage of the Social Security Act, which gave financial support to those who retired.

During the rest of the century, the "retirement age" has increasingly been equated with the onset of "old age," and people at age 65 have been encouraged not only to retire from paid employment, but to withdraw from all active participation in their society.

However, there is increasing evidence that we need a new definition of the mature years, because as average life expectancy lengthened throughout the course of this century, another unexpected development emerged. In addition to living longer, many people were staying physically more vigorous for a longer period of time.

The most dramatic evidence of retarded biological aging is found in a series of studies done over the past twenty years by a Swedish physician, Dr. Alvar Svanborg. Svanborg looked at three successive cohorts of seventy-year-olds, spaced five years apart, at ages 70, 75, and 80. The first cohort has been studied now at all three ages; the second at 70 and 75; and the third for the first time. What has emerged from this study is that each successive cohort is physically "younger," measured in a variety of ways. Most of the persons studied did not get physically "old" until after age 75, and some only in their 80s. This study suggests the possibility that, as life expectancies move closer to the one hundred year mark, the period of vigor for many people may be greatly lengthened as well. We should note here that simultaneously some researchers also voice great concern over what they see as a possible dark side of this development: that the end-of-life period of illness or disability may be lengthened for many people.

All around us we see evidence in real life of increased vitality in the late and middle years of life: people who "retire" in their fifties or sixties to start a new career, become entrepreneurs, study for advanced degrees, or join the Peace Corps. Increasingly, people are inventing new life patterns for themselves, which do not conform to the ideas we have held in the past.

What has begun to develop, in short, is a society in which age 65 is no longer a real watershed point in the individual's physical and professional life. It is for this reason that Alan Pifer, President Emeritus of Carnegie Corporation and Chairman of its Aging Society Project, has proposed a redefinition of the period between the ages of 50 and 75 as the "third quarter of life."

THE "THIRD QUARTER OF LIFE" MODEL

In this model, the first quarter of life, up to age 25, is centered on development and education, and the second, to age 50, on establishing oneself in the work force and community and raising a family.

At about age fifty, another natural transition period is reached. For many people, the early fifties is the time when their children grow up and leave home. If they are members of the labor force, they are likely to have achieved their maximum real earning power in their present jobs and are unlikely to be promoted further. Currently, the possibilities for career change at this age are few. Thus, people often face a choice of staying on at the same job plateau for the next ten to fifteen years or retiring early, finances permitting. It seems that this would be an ideal time to introduce career re-evaluation and change. The concept of the third quarter of life is intended to provide a framework on which to build new policies and practices to develop the productive potential and increase the life satisfaction of people in their fifties and sixties. It represents a full 25 years during which most persons remain relatively healthy and inclined to continue as actively contributing members of their community.

Defining the years between ages 50 and 75 as a new life stage does *not* suggest that everyone should simply be expected to continue in full-time paid employment for an additional ten years to age 75. Just as the tasks of the first and second quarters of life differ from each other, the life patterns that people are evolving for the third quarter are different from those of the earlier quarters. In fact, the concept of the third quarter of life is more descriptive than theoretical. People everywhere seem to be changing their lives and striking out in new directions after age 50, and continuing to explore these pathways for two or three more decades. The kind of productivity people seek out in the third quarter of life seems to be measured in terms of human benefits—providing the services that will maintain and improve the quality of life, and allowing for the individual's maximum sense of growth and well-being. The means for this will certainly span a wide range of working and learning arrangements, including part-time employment, full- and part-time volunteer jobs, and periodic involvement in educational or retraining programs.

There is one more element which should be noted here. It is important to remember, when we talk about people over age 50, that significantly more of them are women than men. About 60% of the over-65 population total, for example, is female, and the female majority increases the older the age group. Women are, in fact, a numerical majority in our population; as the proportion of older persons in the total population grows, so will the female majority. But these patterns of increased activity during the third quarter of life apply to both men and women. In fact, many women who have not had a work life outside the home earlier actually begin to develop a professional career as they approach or enter the third quarter, remaining active for two to four decades—roughly the same length of time as the average man's work life during most of this century.

IMPLICATIONS OF AN AGING SOCIETY
FOR RELIGIOUS INSTITUTIONS

What, then, are the impacts of the aging society on religious institutions?

First of all, the composition of church membership is likely to be markedly different. In the past, churches have been predominantly nuclear-family centered institutions, but they will be less so in the future. Families with children will form a smaller percentage of the overall population; inevitably they will form a smaller percentage of church membership. A larger percentage of the families with children will belong to the black and Hispanic minority groups, which have a tendency toward membership in specifically minority churches. So, there may be an even greater reduction in the family membership in many of the traditionally white, Protestant churches, than appears at first glance.

There will be large numbers of very old people. Traditionally, the very old have seen the church as a source of spiritual comfort and social participation, and probably many will continue to do so. The majority of these older members will be women. Programming for them, meeting their needs, will be a very different proposition than ministering to the needs of families with children. There will also be a number of very old persons whose illness or weakened health will require the kind of services and care that religiously-affiliated institutions have often provided. On the basis of simple demographics, it is safe to predict that there will be a greater need for this kind of care in the future than there has been in the past.

And there will also be an extremely large number of people who are neither young parents nor the truly elderly, but are in the third quarter of life. In just 30 years, by about 2015, *nearly one third of our total population* will be between the ages of 50 and 75. By and large they will be physically vigorous, mentally energetic and active, and possessed of sufficient financial resources to live with reasonable security.

THIRD QUARTER AMERICANS AS A CHALLENGE
TO RELIGIOUS INSTITUTIONS

The one thing these third-quarter Americans—who will begin to be so numerous about twelve years from now—do *not* have is a clearly defined role in our society, for they are a group which has not existed before in their present form. And this is something religious institutions can help to create, if they have the will to do so.

Many third-quarter Americans retire early—in their fifties—from their primary job, not because they want to, or because they have nothing further to contribute to society, but because corporate policy over the last two decades has moved toward pushing people out of the work force earlier and earlier. When the *New York Times* published Alan Pifer's description of the third quarter of life in February, 1984, he was deluged with letters from people in their fifties and sixties who wanted to go on working—whether at a paid job or a volunteer job—but did not know how to find or create this opportunity for themselves.

The emphasis on youth which the Baby Boom years encouraged led us to regard it as the most valuable professional commodity. An "older worker" was synonymous with someone who was rundown, tired, and unproductive, like Willy Loman in "Death of a Salesman." Indeed, Willy Loman is a prime example of how much things have changed in just the last 30 years. Miller's play was written in 1948, and Loman is the archetype of the used-up, exhausted old man, someone who is too old to "make it" anymore in any of the areas of his life. Yet as you read or see the play, you will discover to your surprise that Willy Loman is only *60*.

Clearly it simply is not true now—even if it was true thirty years ago—that most sixty years olds are used up and worn out. Third-quarter Americans are a tremendous reservoir of energy, talent and experience. Churches can create vehicles to help them find new sources of professional activity—channels such as career counseling services and forty plus clubs. And church members in the third quarter can also create programs in which they and other third-quarter Americans can work. Many people in this age group will at some point work at volunteer jobs rather than paid ones. But right now there are few programs which can utilize their talents. We need to look at our society's problems and begin to try to create new program structures which can respond to them.

There is a second major role which churches can play in regard to the third quarter group. Ironically—though it is closer to the traditional role of religion in human life—it will be, I think, more difficult for American churches to fill.

What I mean is the nurturing of individual inner growth, in a mental and emotional sense, and also a spiritual one.

I grew up in the mainstream of middle-American Protestant Christianity, and in a sense, I am relying heavily on personal observation in my speculations at this point. Churches and religious groups in this country by and large have always been organizations which focused more on the *group* than on the *individual.* There is a sense in which we have even been suspicious and disapproving of the individual search for inner knowledge and spiritual growth. One was supposed to be saved, of course, but once that had been accomplished, one was supposed to roll up one's sleeves and get to work, and not too much introspection, thank you.

Perhaps this goes back to the early Puritans' desire to annihilate the self, and replace it with the Divine. Its roots are not clear. But regardless of its origins, it is a pervasive stance. We are uncomfortable about inner growth. There are many casual demonstrations of this which can be cited. Outside New York City, Americans make fun of the preoccupation of New Yorkers with psychotherapy, joking that half the people in New York are residents, and the other half are therapists. We viewed with considerable alarm youth's explorations of altered states, yoga, meditation, EST, and various other self-development systems, during the past two decades. Dan Yankelovich in his book *New Rules* refers with some dismay to the youth of this period as the ''me generation,'' at least in part because of their search for self-knowledge.

But this is a distorted view of what, in my opinion, is a profound, far-reaching, and hope-inspiring phenomenon. Because the key to many human problems can be found within the individual, and in his or her understanding of the self. This is not a new discovery: recognition of this aspect of the human spirit goes back to the origins of Western thought. In his *Apology,* Socrates called knowing oneself the most essential human task after the worship of God. It is the cornerstone upon which all other human exchanges are built. All relationships between people start with the interaction of individuals; all events in the world begin with the individuals who create them. All nations and communities are made up of individuals. If we want to try to eliminate war, and pain, and suffering, we cannot simply depend on the divine will to hand it to us on a platter. We must work toward these things ourselves. And the place to start is with the individual, with ourselves.

I said earlier that I thought it might be more difficult for American religious denominations to meet this inner need than to deal with third quarter Americans' external need for fulfilling work. One reason is the one I have just given—the traditional view in American culture that inner growth is really self-centeredness or narcissism, rather than a normal healthy part of life. The second reason may be partly a result of the first, but it is also a serious handicap. That is, contemporary American Christianity really does not have the means of facilitating and encouraging spiritual growth on an individual basis beyond a very superficial level. Despite all of its many other wonderful and unique characteristics, Christianity is almost completely lacking in the kind of individual growth systems found in some other religious traditions—to give two examples, Zen Buddhism and Hinduism.

During the 1960s, a great many Christians in this country were sorely dismayed to find the country's young people drawn toward Eastern religious practices. There was much interest in yoga and yogic meditation with celebrities such as Timothy Leary and the Beatles making trips to India (and sometimes staying), along with the transplanting of Indian gurus onto American soil and the establishment here and there of Indian-style ashrams. There was Guru Majaraj-ji, who did not last very long here as a guru, and Maharishi Mehesh Yoga, who has lasted and taken root—his transcendental meditation movement has taught hundreds of thousands of Americans to mediate, has generated scientific interest in meditation, and has influenced psychotherapists and physicians in their attitude towards the connections between mind and body.

There has been a similar, though smaller and less publicly visible, interest in Zen Buddhism extending from the '60s to the present, with thousands of people taking up Zen practices and the establishment of Zen centers in various parts of the country.

I believe that the major reason for this is first the phenomenon I just spoke of: that contemporary Christianity is deficient in practices and techniques which foster individual spiritual growth. And second, that *the need for spiritual growth is a biological part of our human nature.*

It is true that, in some respects, spiritual growth can be stimulated by communal activities. But *communal activities alone are not enough.* Any religious group whose entire emphasis is on the communal is bound to run into problems over time.

All of us know that there is immense variety and individuality in this astonishing little world which God created. The example which is conventionally cited is that of snowflakes, all of which are different. On human turf, the scale may be different, but the principle is the same. We human beings are big two-legged snowflakes. We are all different, and so to some extent all of us need to grow and learn and develop spiritually each as an individual.

Longer lives invite reflection; there is more time for it, first of all, and secondly there is more material to work with. Gerontologists, such as Dr. James Birren, Dean of the Andrus Center at the University of Southern California, have developed a number of techniques, such as autobiographical and life review methods, which enable the individual to probe and assimilate his or her life experience. Modern psychology has come into its own, with a range of techniques for inner growth which are truly remarkable. There are a number of human development systems such as DMA, EST and self-actualization which have been created in this country over the past twenty years. They provide extremely effective modes of getting in touch with the deeper levels of the self and of working to change one's life constructively.

My surmise is that the third-quarter group may be deeply drawn to this kind of inner search. Partly this is based on history—many of the gerontological techniques were developed and have been used primarily with people in the third quarter—and partly it is based on the personal observation that many people now engaged in such work are close to or in their third quarter. Churches can serve as a logical focal point for such learning, if they are willing to do so—if they are willing to see it as the basis for a deeply integrated, inner spirituality rather than a navel-gazing experience which diminishes conformity to the external, social rules of religion; and if they understand that it is a movement toward positive growth, rather than a manifestation of selfishness. Basically, I am suggesting a life span development approach to spirituality, instead of our old mode, which used to hold the belief that once you're grown up you're finished, and you can't and don't need to grow any more.

CONCLUSION

Many commentators on age over the past several years have appeared to be alarmed about the extension of life which our society has achieved, and about the presence of so many older Americans in our population mix. I confess that I am not one of those. Every advance in human knowledge represents an opportunity to use the results well or badly. We now have a tremendous opportunity, both individually and collectively, to use this newly minted life stage. It is up to us to use it well.

Aging and the Dimensions
of Spiritual Development

William M. Clements, M.Div., Ph.D.

ABSTRACT. The human spirit has personal and corporate dimensions and can enjoy experiential continuity, with growth and/or regression on both levels at any point in the life-cycle. *Memory* and *prolepsis* contribute to spiritual development—memory by transmitting the past and bestowing identity, prolepsis by incorporating a vision of the future into the present—thereby making creativity possible. Society's view of time can preclude a vision of the future appropriate for spiritual development in old age; however, the future can be viewed as a series of discrete moments, allowing the creativity necessary for spiritual development. The role of the church in spiritual development is vital on both the popular and the basic levels. Two concrete proposals are presented.

This discussion of the "dimensions of spiritual development" makes four basic presuppositions. (1) There is something called *the human spirit* and that it is possible to have intelligible and meaningful discussions about the human spirit. (2) The human spirit may be considered to have a personal, or private, dimension, and a corporate, or collective, dimension. (3) The human spirit, whether personal or corporate, has the capacity and the need to enjoy experiential continuity through time. There is a reflexive quality about the human spirit that enables self-awareness to emerge at various points in the life cycle or the historical process. (4) The human spirit can both grow and regress on an individual level of existence and also on the corporate level of history.

Many factors contribute to spiritual development. I want to highlight two for our consideration. The first is *memory*. The second is *prolepsis*. Then I will make two concrete proposals for action.

William M. Clements is Director of Behavioral Science and Pastoral Counselor in the Department of Family Practice at The Medical Center, P.O. Box 951, Columbus, Georgia 31994, and Associate Professor of Community Medicine, Emory University, Atlanta, Georgia.

127

The two concrete ideas will be examined in the light of the *role of the church in spiritual development.* Much of what I will say is intensely personal because I believe that spiritual development *is* intensely personal on the individual level. At the same time, there is that corporate aspect, which I will also try to address.

MEMORY

Can civilization, much less full personhood, exist without *memory*? If all the memory banks in all of the computers were down at the same time that all of the books and all of the manuscripts were inaccessible and if all individual human beings experienced amnesia at the same time, would civilization exist in any meaningful way? I think not. The capacity *to remember* is the collagen, or connective tissue, of civilization. It is unseen and taken for granted. Memory is the connective tissue that binds discrete moments together and gives humanity the sense of continuity that is so vital to civilization and to persons within society.

Memory has real historical antecedents and affects the outcome of present realities. Not long ago I was driving my octogenarian mother to Columbus, Georgia, for a brief visit. As we were traveling along, my mother mentioned that her ankles had begun to swell again. Earlier in the day I had noticed a slight wheezing in her breathing as we carried items to load in the car. I was fascinated by the problem that these symptoms represented. Not the medical problem of congestive heart failure, nor the diuretic treatment so carefully prescribed by my late father's former medical partner. These were known aspects of the situation. The problem that fascinated me was different from that.

As the hills and trees slowly passed along the country roads, I thought to myself, "Why does Mother have a problem taking her medicine?" After all, more than half a century ago she had married the young, scientifically trained physician who was known in the community as the "pee" doctor because he examined urine with a microscope. His colleagues in the community were "buggy doctors" in that they had travelled in a buggy with another physician to get their training. For almost fifty years, Mother had made housecalls with my father and had participated vicariously in the observance of the emergence of modern laboratory medicine. Something didn't add up.

I knew that Mother is getting a little forgetful about recent details. I also knew that she is fiercely compensating by making lists of things to remember. She has one of those seven-day capsule containers and had no trouble keeping her medication straight when she had an infection and was taking antibiotics. As I drove along, I mumbled something like, "You seem to be having a little trouble with that medicine." She looked at me with a knowing glance and started to tell me why.

We never were much to take medicine in my family, growing up. When someone went to the doctor in those days, they were really sick. Morris went when he broke his arm cranking the car to go to church one Sunday morning. The doctor came to our house when George Will was just a tyke and into the medicine or poison or something and went blind.

I only remember my father getting sick once. He must have had the flu or something. He was in bed and under the covers and Mother couldn't get him to take any medicine. She called me out on the back porch and whispered to me to "go and get Grandpa." Grandpa lived just down the street where Uncle Ed used to live. Well, I went and got Grandpa Turner. He came back with me and walked into Daddy's room and put his hand on my father's head and stood back saying, "Will, you are sick. I'm going to fix you some medicine." Grandpa went into the kitchen and proceeded to stir loudly the glass of liquid medicine Mother had already tried to get Daddy to take. He brought it back into the bedroom and said, "Here, Willie, take this." Dad sat up in bed like a little boy and drank his medicine, and Grandpa went home. That was that. The Turners have never really taken much medicine.

I learned something important about by mother's attitude toward taking medicine for sure. But I learned something else about my grandfather, Will Turner, who died in 1917, nearly thirty years before I was born. Obviously, I never met Will Turner in person, but I honestly feel like I know him. His personality, his approach to life, and even his mannerisms were lovingly transmitted to me over the years. Perhaps I know him better than if I had experienced him directly for myself, because only the important things about him were told over the years at family gatherings. In a real sense, the memory of Will Turner, whom I never met, has had a significant influence on the person I have become. My identity, in part, has been shaped by the memories of this man, dead for nearly seventy years.

My point is not only that memory often explains present behavior, which it does, but also that *memory bestows identity.* My identity does not come only from those events directly experienced by me. Identity also comes from those memories that have been given to me by others. As in the case of Will Turner taking his medicine eighty years ago, who I am today is determined not only by what I have directly experienced for myself, or by those precious memories that have been transmitted to me. In a similar fashion, the memories of the church have been lovingly transmitted from generation to generation. Jesus Christ, as living memory, is proclaimed and represented in such a way that Christian identity is formed and enhanced throughout the human life-cycle.

Present identity is also determined by *which accounts of history* I have chosen to read or hear and have appropriated into a personal frame of reference. For identity to emerge there needs to be a degree of continuity in regard to outer events and the inner appropriation of those events. Some degree of sameness needs to be present between one moment and the next so that the patterns of connectedness can be established in consciousness, and organization or form can be given. Persons, families and institutions all embody in one form or another these memories that are constructed into identities.

The memories of those patterns or habits of thinking that shape our lives are not always accessible even to our conscious awareness. As I read and reread John Farina's account of Isaac Hecker, in *An American Experience of God* (Ramsey, N.J.: Paulist Press, 1981), this point became abundantly clear. Briefly, Isaac Hecker was born to a Methodist mother in New York in 1819. He remained unconfirmed yet under the tutelage of this denomination until he drifted away around the age of fifteen. Thereafter, he experimented with a variety of religious orientations, including Transcendentalism, in his quest for a church home that reflected his inner faith. At thirty years of age he felt that his spiritual quest had led him in a radically different direction as he joined the Roman Catholic Church and eventually founded the Missionary Society of St. Paul the Apostle. Hecker's conscious decision, he felt, had led him a different direction from the Protestantism of his mother; yet Farina repeatedly points out how the major themes of Hecker's ministry were largely prefigured in the faith he had intended to leave behind. So deeply do the roots of memory sink that one does not always even have to remember consciously in order to be influenced by patterns of meaning from the past.

Religious communities are the historical embodiments of a particular set of memories and stories that have been handed from generation to generation. I learned this very dramatically during my first semester as a student at Union Seminary. Professor Cyril Richardson had just spent an entire hour in Church History explaining in minute detail the intricacies of one of the early controversies in what was becoming the Christian Church. The controversy between those who believed that Christ had two natures, one human and one divine, and those who believed that Christ had only one nature raged on and on. Then, of course, the winners branded the losers as heretics and that was that. At the end of the lecture, Professor Richardson asked if there were any questions. A student sitting three seats from me raised his hand. Professor Richardson called on the student, who said something like, "You have done an admirable job explaining this controversy from the Western viewpoint. However, I am a Nestorian priest and we explain the issues a little differently." The student then gave an equally detailed explanation of the Nestorian view of the matter. From that small event I learned much about perspective and the importance of tradition, very little of which, however, had to do with the nature of the Nestorian "heresy," the details of which escape me.

There can be no identity in a religious sense without memory. The words, "I am the Lord your God who led you out of the land of Egypt" and "After supper he took the cup and blessed it and said, 'Do this in remembrance of me,'" make memory a present reality and simultaneously confer identity on the participants. *Spiritual development requires an identity and identity comes from memory.*

PROLEPSIS

A second important component of spiritual development is that of *prolepsis,* which is the assumption of a future act or a development as if it presently exists or has already been accomplished. For prolepsis even to exist with regard to spiritual development there must exist a hopeful vision of the future that serves as a growthful lure in the present. We see prolepsis most clearly embodied in the Eucharist. During the Eucharist, we are not merely looking back and remembering a past event as present reality, we are also looking forward and *anticipating* as present reality. The hope of the eschatological banquet is experienced as a foretaste in the Eucharist.

All too often, however, the prolepsis that exists in old age is only that of regression or stagnation. Our society does not have a vision of old age as a time of spiritual development. This is a paradox because examples of spiritual growth in the last decades of life abound on all sides, yet the vision of growthful existence by a Mother Teresa, or a John Wesley, or a Pope John XXIII, never gets translated into popular culture. That vision of an old age with the possibility of spiritual development somehow has remained inaccessible to ordinary people.

TIME

Perhaps part of the explanation for this deficit lies in the consensus definition of time that seems to be operative in our culture. How we utilize and experience the notion of time is so basic to existence that most of us for most of our days live without reflecting on or even considering the nature and meaning of time. The concepts of time that I experience have for me a visual and an imaginative quality about them that I would like for *you* to experience for yourself. Visually, imagine yourself standing on a vast, level plain that stretches before you and behind you farther than your eye can see. Imagine that you have a gigantic ball of string beside you that you can roll across the plain, leaving a line of string from your present position to the point at which you wish to stop. If you roll the ball in the direction behind you, you go backward in history. If you roll the ball in front of you, you go forward in time. Now it seems to me that our society, with this sort of linear, clock time, believes that the notion of "future" refers only to the *distant* future, and that the notion of "history" refers only to the distant past. As a result of this notion of time, people who become aware of nearing a finite limit to how far their personal balls of string can be rolled forward act as if, in the absence of a distant future, there is *no* future at all. Experientially, for them there is no future that is worth pursuing. In such a scheme of meaning the string being unrolled ahead does not go anywhere. There is no forward movement. There is no vision of future directivity.

Contrast this linear notion of time with one that is more "present" oriented. Imagine again that you are on the vast plain. This time, instead of a ball of string, you have a Polaroid camera. You turn around and take a picture behind you. As the photo grinds out of the camera, you are surprised to see that it shows you in the act of turning, for this is a very special camera. You catch a glimpse of the photo behind that one and it shows you checking the film in your camera. You turn and look ahead and take a picture. It shows you laying the camera aside, and the one in front of that shows you placing the camera in the case. With this conception of time, the photo that comes out of the camera facing rearward is past time, and the photo that emerges facing forward is future time. Each photo represents a discrete moment of time that is distinguishable from the photo in front, and from the one in back, yet is obviously related to both. My conception is that creativity on the personal level emerges in the gap between your present position and the photo that is nearest to you in front. Creativity, when it comes, does not relate to the distant future. On the personal level the distant future is fantasy. The moment of creative insight, or synthesis, is happening as discrete photos of the near future are being formed so that there is still an opportunity to influence the context of the photo. The creative moment is happening when the future moment exists as possibility, not quite yet reality; when the future moment exists as a glimpse, not a certainty.

What you hope to see in that fleeting moment as you catch a glimpse is all important. If you close your eyes, then that action has an influence on your sense of excitement and an influence on your directivity. If you look to the distant future and see nothing, then that action, too, has an influence on the emergence of personal creativity.

The prolepsis of the moment is the moment of spiritual development. Spiritual development is happening *in this moment* of leaping into the future, or it is not happening at all. What you hope to see influences where you land, or to continue our image, what sort of photo emerges from your camera of meaning. It takes an act of faith to believe in the *not quite yet* that enables the vision of growth to emerge into reality.

The content of the vision will be different for each person. It will be more specific than general. The important point is not the question, "What is the image that allows spiritual development to take place?" because there are many images, but rather, "What is the *process*?" And then, "How can this process be facilitated in the religious community and in society at large?"

ROLE OF THE CHURCH

The role of the church in spiritual development is a vital role. No other institution in society can perform this function. The church needs to deploy self-consciously resources on both *the popular level* and *the basic level* to begin emphasizing the opportunities for spiritual development in our society. Any effort must involve a high degree of cooperation among religious institutions and needs to deal effectively with the popular culture *and* emerging generations of religious leaders during their period of formation.

Proposal I

Specifically, on the level of popular culture, churches need to band together in a concerted effort to make available *religious biography* of heroes of the faith who were themselves embarking upon significant spiritual developments in the latter decades of life. Such biographies need to transcend narrow denominational triumphalism, becoming, instead, universal in their appeal to the human spirit. Such biographies need to be easily accessible to ordinary people and might include stories in popular commercial literature, Sunday School lessons and discussion group starters, sermonic material, as well as audiovisual presentations that appeal to viewers of commercial television. The languages of faith are many and the church's task of interpretation is vitally important. Any attempt to facilitate the emergence of directivity in society must involve popular culture and must involve a cooperative effort among varied religious traditions.

Proposal II

In contrast to the religious biography project that impacts popular culture, a different strategy needs to be employed when dealing with basic professional issues that impact theological education. The most basic issue in theological education is the lack of an adequate knowledge base in gerontology. Here I am not thinking so much of cannibalizing extant gerontological knowledge and sprinkling it across theological education, although this is an admirable goal. What is needed instead is the creation of a discipline such as *religious gerontology,* in which persons already highly trained in church history, theology, biblical studies, ethics, pastoral care and counseling, homiletics and religious education, and already deployed as tenured professors in seminaries and departments of religion are enabled to develop the gerontological knowledge base *within religion* that is so vital to the education of future generations of religious leaders.

What is so desperately needed is the creation of an adequately funded program offering postdoctoral fellowships in religious gerontology for tenured faculty who hold unusual promise for success in scholarship and publication. Such a creative and dynamic program could draw together in one setting scholars and teachers from divergent academic, theological, ethnic and geographic backgrounds who would pursue independent graduate study in secular gerontology while they simultaneously developed the knowledge bases within their own disciplines in regard to aging issues.

Over the course of the full-time fellowship year, fellows would participate in integrative seminars and each would develop a research paper or course syllabus that demonstrated either new knowledge or the integration of extant gerontological knowledge in regular discipline courses taught by fellows in their institutional homes. Then, at the conclusion of the fellowship year, participants would serve as the faculty for a continuing education institute designed to reach religious professionals who already serve elderly people.

Several positive outcomes may result from such a program. After a number of classes have completed the fellowship program, a database called *religious gerontology* will have been developed. Perhaps a self-perpetuating field of study or interest will have been nurtured into existence. It may be hoped that fellows will involve graduate students in research at the intersection formed between their disciplines and human aging. As fellows return to their positions as tenured faculty, they will bolster the course offerings that have authentic religious gerontology in traditional courses. Since fellows will have already taught one new course incorporating the knowledge and skills of their respective disciplines with a new sensitivity and awareness of human aging, other additions in content are likely to occur as well. This continuing process over time will help to reduce the widespread deficit in gerontological content found in the traditional theological disciplines. The summer continuing education institute, with the fellows as faculty, will gradually help to reduce the deficit in knowledge and skills among persons already working in professional capacities.

As a result of this program of fellowships in religious gerontology, new knowledge and skills will become available in local communities across the country. As new generations of religious professionals take their places in positions of community leadership, imaginative and appropriate directivity will emerge—a directivity in which spiritual development across the life span is *the* glimpse of the future that lends depth and meaning to each succeeding moment.

Toward New Directions
for Ministry in Aging:
An Overview of Issues and Concepts

Arden K. Barden, M.Th.

ABSTRACT. The church has a leadership role in the field of aging in providing its own definitions, utilizing its own resources, and functioning with the spiritual orientation toward person-centered growth of the aging. While psycho-social theories of aging have shaped the church's role in the past, the church should avoid ageism, broadly define aging, and reinterpret its functions. The themes of religiosity, religion, theology, spirituality, and ministry are discussed. The developmental and wholistic goal of the church's involvement in aging is spiritual well-being. Solid theological basis and careful spiritual focus lead to sound ministry. Development of the concept of spiritual aging is proposed.

INTRODUCTION

The church's struggle to define its role in aging must begin with the realization that the bulk of the body of information in the field has come from the physical and human sciences. The definitions of age-related terms and the usage of church-related words have been determined largely by the students of biology, psychology, and sociology. Multidisciplinary approaches in gerontology often include only biological, psychological, and sociological aging, omitting spiritual-religious factors. Existing church responses to concerns in aging have followed the lead of these disciplines, particularly as shaped by the activity and disengagement theories of aging. As a minister studying gerontology, my observation is that there is a serious deficiency of theological input into the meaning of and responses to aging. That becomes the underlying issue in the church-and-aging discussion.

Arden K. Barden is Pastor, Terrace Heights Lutheran Church, 3605 Hillcroft Way, Yakima, Washington 98901.

The roles of the church in aging will be shaped by the questions we ask, and the focus of those questions will need to be the church's task of spiritual care and biblical witness in the context of the faith-in-life experiences of the aging. Who are the aging persons for whom and with whom we strive to define our involvement? Is aging a determined but struggling effort to stay involved in life, a calculated but uncontrollable withdrawal from life, or a natural but growing process toward meaning for life? At what point in the aging process is there a call for unique applications of ministry, or, ought ministry to be perceived differently in its meaning, function and purpose throughout the life span? Where do faith's fundamentals as known in our biblical and ecclesiastical heritage fit in understanding and approaching aging persons? What is our message and mission regarding aging in personal concerns, policy development and community life? To answer those kinds of questions, we will need to remember who we are and why we are here, based on the study of our theological resources of biblical story and imagery, church history and events, and contemporary witness and experience.

We the church have before us an opportunity to provide leadership in the field of aging because our calling (or role) in this instance is to serve aging persons in the context of the unique aspects of the human experience which are certainly posed by, potentially confronted within, and hopefully enhanced through, the aging process itself. Further, the leadership potential of the church's spiritual-religious discussions and programs is optimally stimulated by utilizing our own resources rather than following the cues of other disciplines; our participation as a church in prophetic and priestly ministry by nature implies an ongoing struggle for appropriate involvement in policy and planning within the socio-political milieu as well as a continuing presence in caring and sharing with aging persons; and the church's creativity in aging strategically opens the opportunity not only for clarification of existing information but perhaps also for the shaping of new directions for ministry and aging.

AGING, AGING THEORY, AND AGEISM
IN THE CHURCH

To begin with the agenda of aging persons is to begin with some self-examination about our use of aging-related terminology. I use the term "aging" to reflect the broader, more inclusive aspects of the field, such as demographics and life changes, bio-psycho-social studies, historical-cultural aspects, political-environmental themes, individual and interpersonal dynamics, and, of course, spiritual matters. Aging is a process that takes place in persons and that both affects and is affected by those diverse aspects of age-related human experience. Persons, however, become designated as old people, the old, elders, the elderly, senior citizens, and the aged, sometimes to the dissatisfaction and unpleasant experiences of those persons involved. To select any one label or to choose any one criterion as a characteristic or primary sense of aging is to do an injustice to the complex and interrelated facets of aging, and thus to aging persons. Certainly, we will need to be very cautious regarding our own ageism as it would occur through focusing on age and decline. Naming and defining people by some secularly proposed categories of chronological standards, functional ability, health status, socioeconomic patterns, or cultural stereotypes, may skew our vision for and relationship with persons in need of our leadership and our ministry. The risks are that we would prejudge and discriminate the aging into minority group status, that we would produce exclusiveness when we seek inclusiveness, and that we would create emotional or spiritual distance when we seek genuine ministry.

To support the dignity and potential of each aging human being, I have come to prefer the broad reference of the phrase ''the aging'' (Clements, 1981). Aging discussions for the church and its role begin with people. The aging are those persons involved in the aging process. The aging are those for whom the process has become evident in their own lives, either by self-awareness and self-definition or by societal, cultural or environmental determinations. Precise definitions and dehumanized categories may be helpful to measurement and analysis for the scientific process but they are not conducive to the creative response by the church for person-centered, inclusive ministry enabled by genuine caring and inspired by spiritual considerations. A review of aging theories (cf. Weiner, Brok and Snadowsky, 1978) will help to assess the validity of that statement.

The physical science view of the body as a machine has led to the notion that, even though every machine has its limits and eventually wears out, if used and maintained the body-machine will endure throughout its time span of service. The aging process is thus one of appropriate physical and mental wear and tear with an emphasis on remaining active with careful choices for well-being as the way to healthy aging. The church with other segments of society has responded to this activity theory by creating all kinds of programs designed to keep aging persons involved. Crafts, luncheons, trips, voluntarism, and the like (Fecher, 1982; Clingan, 1975; Sessoms, 1977; Maves, 1981) are considered to be the meaningful response to the needs of the aging. The assumption is that the older people become, the more concern that they need to be involved. The role faith plays is literally to find ways to live and to affirm life throughout the aging process, and it is the church's role to help provide this involvement. Since decline and death reflect defeat, they are thus counteracted with a determined expression of activity as a means of victoriously asserting life and activity in the face of the experiences of aging.

A contrary view of the physical sciences is that the human body has a limited amount of energy which is expended over time, and, like a clock, it simply runs down. The slower movement at the end of the time span calls for an adjustment to decreased roles and a preparation for the eventual stopping. Aging is guided disengagement from purposeful physical, psychological and social involvement. The assumption is that the older people become, the more they prefer to be left alone and need only periodic assistance to adjust in the course of their decline. The church with other segments of society has responded with programs that enable older adults to be alone, but, of course, not forgotten. Media programs, telephone contacts, pastoral counseling, and lay or pastoral visitation (Fecher, 1982; Brown, 1964; Gray and Moberg, 1962) are common efforts which intend to supportively help people to withdraw and prepare for decline to the point of death. A significant amount of literature deals with faith, death anxiety, grief and aging (Gray and Moberg, 1962; LeFevre and LeFevre, 1981). Losses of spouse, friends, home, belongings, and health are interpreted as difficult but natural and necessary encounters in the process of aging. As aging occurs the role of faith becomes a more appropriate factor in adjustment, particularly regarding a belief in the afterlife. The church's role is to provide that kind of religious experience which facilitates acceptance as losses occur and as death approaches. Disengagement from this world's roles is thus counteracted with engagement in next world hopes.

There are two issues here. The first has to do with the participation of the church in cultural values which assign higher value to sexual attractiveness or youthfulness, personal power or fame, and individual achievement or productivity. We may presume that the values of the post-World War II affluent society are what informed the studies of aging in the 1940s and 1950s. Not only was purity of scientific method the goal, but also there was the backdrop of peacetime production and growth. Undergirded by applications of the northern European (young, white, male) Protestant work ethic, human life became valued more directly in terms of health, hard work and productivity, such that people of color, the older age groups, those with disabilities, and women were implicitly regarded as less than fully human. There should be little wonder that the studies of those periods would find correlations of age, decline, loss, and separation (therefore natural aging as disengagement) or of age, ability, activity, positive attitude, and involvement (therefore natural aging as activity). In addition, these findings came at a time when the numbers of survivors into later years were increasing, seemingly highlighting the findings and pointing to the validity of these theories for understanding aging. With increasing age people were seen as either settling back to eternal rewards for a job well done, or continuing with as much stamina as possible actively involved in work alternatives with similar positive achievements and experiences while here on earth.

The second issue is that those theories have been the source of the church's information about the aging. Adopting the world's standards, so to speak, the church developed its concern accordingly for the aging in its membership. One might question, however, the meaning of explicitly bringing a visit and a word of life while implicitly acknowledging and even assisting in the power of decline and death. One might want to rethink the significance of programs that have as a primary goal keeping people busy while perhaps facilitating a form of denial of aging. One might evaluate the true value of calling on people to show they are cared for while helping them keep their preapproved distance from genuine involvement, or of insisting upon their attendance at a variety of programs which below the surface have the potential of lacking real purpose and content beyond the attendance records. The church's roles in aging in these contexts have been measured by numbers of people served, especially relative to minimal budget expenditures. The various aspects of the numbers game have perhaps contributed to an insensitivity toward the needs of individual aging persons as well as having likewise failed to render meaningful ministry for their lives.

A third trend in the theories of aging is that of the growth and developmental interpretation of the life span in which change is accepted and expected throughout life stages. Ironically, at the same time disengagement and activity were emerging as interpretations of aging in the United States, the language of life meaning, life fulfillment, and natural individuation was emerging on the continent (cf. Charlotte Buhler and C. J. Jung summarized in Weiner et al., 1978; cf. Frankl, 1959, 1971). Such themes became the foundation of humanistic psychology and the human potential movement as, in turn, aging theory has been enhanced by Erickson's stages, expanded by Peck's detailing, and applied by Butler's life review process and Kübler-Ross's death and dying descriptions (Weiner et al., 1978).

While the physical science basis is one which views even physical existence as having mystical quality, the key is the appreciation of aging as a natural and "healthy" development and maturation in the human experience. Implicit therefore is the recognition of aging persons as worthy of affirmation, support and meaning throughout continuous change and growth as human beings. The church and other segments of society have more recently developed some response to the aging process based on this perspective of human aging (Fecher, 1982; Reichert and Reichert, 1976; Clements, 1981; McClellan, 1977; LeFevre and LeFevre, 1981). Characteristic differences are observed in more obvious and intentional concerns for the whole person in contrast to primarily a physical or psycho-social emphasis, making self-determined choices in contrast to adapting to or avoiding the inevitable, quality of life in addition to quantity, meaning for life rather than simply preparation for death, sense of community instead of the extremes of isolation or busyness, and the sense of self and inner spirituality as opposed to the more scientifically measured attributes.

Although developmental theories and paradigms may appear more compatible with a person-centered focus and inclusive ministry goals, the church will need to continue to remind itself of its identity, resources and purposes. The temptation, for example, may be to take the described outcomes of Erickson's stages as normative for development and to apply religious meanings in defining the church's role in aging. While dialog with the human sciences will necessarily continue as the information about the human experience expands, the role the church chooses must rather be formed out of its own contexts.

DEFINING THE CHURCH'S ROLE IN AGING

Regarding the gerontological view of the church's role and of spiritual-religious factors in aging, there is presently a blending of terminology. Words that represent church-related functioning are used somewhat interchangeably and seemingly without any order or movement from one to the other. Although some authors have maintained distinctions (Moberg, 1971), the church will need to guide these various aspects of the spiritual-religious discussion by giving them its own definitions and structure. The desired outcomes are an open relationship of clarified roles and mutual respect with the human sciences and a recognized channel for the church's participation in the field of aging. The following five themes are important as a basis for considering the church's role in aging: religiosity, religion, theology, spirituality, and ministry. While they may overlap, they ought not to be confused, and they need to be recognized for their respective contribution to the discussion.

Religiosity may be defined as *the degree and type of religious expression and participation of the aging.* These mannerisms must be operationally definable, specific, measurable, and consistent (cf. Moberg, 1968). They may be studied in relation to selected social and personality factors to determine the presence or absence of correlations across age groups in a given time or of the same cohort over a span of time. Studies in religiosity have been used to assess significant contributory or detrimental factors relative to presumed successful aging as disengagement, activity, or development. In discussing the role of the church in aging, such data are useful as descriptive information of aging concerns or as helpful feedback for program evaluation, but they should not be regarded as predictive for situations of ministry or determinative for the church's role. Nevertheless, continued dialog about the dynamics of religiosity and aging will enhance general understanding and enable improved services for the aging (cf. *Generations,* 1983; Tilberg, 1984).

Religion may be defined as *the structuring and institutionalizing of spiritual-religious interests into worship ritual, moral code, doctrinal definitions, professed commitment, and organizational systems.* Religion includes both individual and corporate beliefs, practices and programs. Religious programmatic design and implementation has been equated with ''the ministry'' and has been the primary content of the church's response to the aging. A review of programs reveals that religious efforts have often followed the indicated needs of the aging according to psycho-social theory and studies. Religious books and articles (Fecher, 1982) have related to one or more of a few major themes, again largely following human science designations: information on the aged or agency; visitation for the shut-in or homebound; program development; biblical or theological rationale for involvement in programmatic ministry to the aging; and in more recent years, the concept of spiritual well-being, although the relevant substance of many of the recommendations of religion and spiritual well-being segments of the White House conferences has also been programmatically oriented. In sum, the role of the church in aging has been regarded in the context of religious programming and organizational involvement, and attempts to break out of that mold to more dynamic interpretations of theology, spirituality and ministry in aging have been repressed by other trends in the American socio-political arena.

The question in determining the church's role in aging is, from where does the church receive its information, inspiration, and motivation? Since the church has unique resources and procedures, it is proposed that theology is the proper context for beginning to discern the role of the church in aging. *Theology* may be defined as *the task of developing from spiritual-religious resources meaningful and dynamic images and perspectives that are instructive and inspirational for interpreting and living the human experience.* It may involve a more phenomenological approach to life experience, the fine arts, and religious traditions. For the Judeo-Christian heritage that means utilizing the rich resources and revelations of biblical writings and historical tradition as well as reflecting upon the ongoing struggle of human aging (Moberg, 1971; Nouwen and Gaffney, 1976; Hiltner, 1975; Thorson and Cook, 1980; LeFevre and LeFevre, 1981; Clements, 1981). It will mean studying aging experiences and aged persons in those resources but it will also mean studying other meanings of spiritual-religious language, relationships and events and drawing from them to provide imagery and meanings that address the concerns of today's aging. Theology studies the resources of the church while keeping in focus those whom the church is called to serve, in this case, the aging.

Spirituality is the context and spiritual well-being the goal for the theological and ministry tasks. *Spirituality* may be defined as *the realm of inner-human, interhuman, and beyond-human dynamics which integrates and gives meaning to all of human experience.* Theology in aging gives meaning to life and life to meaning—

theology shapes spirituality in aging-related human experience. Since spirituality happens in, among and between human beings as well as in relation to the divine, *spiritual well-being* may be defined as *personal and social wholeness that enables the individual to fully respond to (or be present to) his or her God, self, neighbor, and world.* To be spiritual is to have the ability to be a responsive, relating person, a "living being" of Genesis 2:7; that is, one who is able to deeply worship and obey one's God (as understood in that person's belief system), to freely receive and give life from within the self, to openly create and sustain relationships of love with other human beings, and to responsibly utilize and care for one's natural and human made environment.

For the church as a part of Judeo-Christian spirituality, perhaps the best guide for assessing spiritual well-being is *shalom.* Personal and social wholeness means *peace* in its deepest and richest sense: the fullness of life which is the state of living in harmony with all humanity, having financial prosperity, good health, peace of mind, and the free growth of the inner soul. From God, in Christ, through the Holy Spirit, the human person inhales the very spirit or wind of life that pervades the human experience and integrates all its aspects, giving the meaning, power and uniqueness of human individuality. Indeed, in Christian understanding, the spiritual well-being of human spirituality is what makes the human being like God, responsive to God, and representative of God.

The implication of spirituality and spiritual well-being for the role of the church in aging is that the church is not limited to or bound by religious language and religious practice. Its focus is not simply God-centered words, experiences and structures and its identifying characteristics are not those prescribed in the observed activities of historical religiosity. Rather the focus is person-centered within the human experience and of necessity is wholistic in nature. (cf. Tournier, 1957, 1972). The words, relationships and events of God's Word incarnate in scripture, history and the present human struggle serve as the church's resources for relating to all the unique aspects of aging-related human experience. Spiritual well-being as the hoped for outcome of the church's role in aging can be nothing less than as simply if even unscientifically (Moberg, 1979) defined in 1975 by the National Interfaith Coalition on Aging (cf. Thorson and Cook, 1980, p. xiii): "The affirmation of life in a relationship with God, self, community and environment that nurtures and celebrates wholeness."

If as a church we have acknowledged the study of faith-related experiences (religiosity) and accepted that there are aspects of those experiences that are defined and structured (religion), and if as a church we identify and use our own resources (theology) and with them define our own context and goals (spirituality and spiritual well-being) for the role of the church in aging, then it remains to apply spiritual imagery and perspective within everyday needs, problems and opportunities of aging persons; in short, ministry in aging. *Ministry* may be defined as *the enhancement of personal meaning and quality of life for any human being regarding one or more aspects of spiritual well-being.* In the context of the role of the church in aging, ministry means bringing the faith of the Judeo-Christian tradition to bear within the lives of the aging. It is no less than the unfolding through spiritual imagery and human relationship "the Way, the Truth, and the Life" for the aging person.

Thus, ministry may be at one of two levels: a deeper reflective level of meaning and integration of the human experience, or a broader practical level of direct needs and objectives of human existence. The first enables development of the core of spirituality within the experience of human aging; the second supports the maintenance or advancement of all facets of well-being throughout the aging process. Further, the range of ministry experiences includes the silent presence of "just being there," teaching and devotional insight, spiritual therapy and counseling, ancillary services, affirming involvement of the aging person, and major socioeconomic policies and projects. And, although ministry occurs through certain planned as well as spontaneous situations, we must remember that it is not the named experience or project itself that is the ministry, but rather the empowerment, affirmation, sharing of life, and other spiritual meaning or growth that occurs through the particular situation.

AN ILLUSTRATION OF THE CHURCH'S ROLE

The above concerns may be illustrated by the following example. As I was vacationing this summer, I noticed the great number of helpful roadside rest areas which are designed for a variety of activities to accommodate the needs of the traveler toward relief of one sort or another. That "pause that refreshes" also applies to rest breaks in the workplace and in the classroom, although the room in which we rest is not always the rest room. We also get away for a longer rest in the change of place and pace that is vacationing itself. It is interesting to me that in our culture resting takes on meaning primarily in contrast to work-defined activity. The goal of the stopping or reprieve is to find relief and refreshment in order to get back to the activity, to "hit it" again. It is not always a positive connotation as it may indicate a lack of strength or endurance, a frustration with the task at hand, or a failure in ability to achieve the desired results. Consider, too, how some people's recreation or leisure time is more an action-filled busyness than a time of rest and re-creation—in our society, we do not like to have to rest. And, in another sense, there is even the sense of exclusion, of being left out, left over, left behind, or left alone when being a part of "the rest" means the remainder, the one still there after the names of the others are called into participation. With the aging, rest becomes even more negative because the demand for rest confronts the fact that there are activities and groups to which one cannot return. Aging persons bemoan the increased need for rest and fear the isolation of remaining while others either have gone on to their just rewards or are going on with daily life. In keeping with good psycho-social theory, we try to console those who must rest more often or we challenge others to keep going without rest. No one, of course, wants to go to a rest home; no one wants to be left alone to do nothing, to rest all the time; and, certainly no one is wishing for the final resting place and decay unto total nothingness!

If we detach ourselves from activity and disengagement theory and the influence of cultural designations, and begin with theological understandings, we discover meanings that may contribute to spiritual well-being which we may then offer through ministry in the context of human aging. Theologically, rest has to do with completion, satisfaction, fulfillment and celebration. The ones "remaining" are not misfits and has-beens relative to their culture and religion; rather they are the faithful remnant for whom and through whom there is enhanced meaning and purpose in life; indeed, a special identity and mission. Similarly, God did not cease from the work of creation as an exhausted and discouraged God who had spent all eternal energy and who wondered what was happening next. Rather, the creator felt a sense of pleasure and fulfillment at the ultimate self-expression of the word—It is good (Genesis 1 and 2). It was in appreciation and celebration that out of the creative word would flow the redeeming word and the life-giving word as

God's total investment in all that is said and done would bring ultimate joy and eternal satisfaction; in short, "the *rest* of life"; that is,
the rest which *is* life. Only hardened unbelief and spiritual disobedi-
ence will prevent us humans from entering that rest of God (Psalm
95). Yet it is also that rest to which we are invited through the saving
Christ relationship as it is offered as a gift (Matthew 11:25-30), free
of charge from the yoke of Christ as over against the burdens and
uncertainties of the daily round under human expectations and
human failings. And it is that rest that is the promised land of untold
blessedness, meaningfulness and fulfillment toward which life itself
moves to perfection and completion (Hebrews 3 and 4). Indeed, the
faithful "rest" are not "alone," and through waiting only on the
Lord, those last shall be the first to enjoy the rest that is to be revealed.

Human aging at all ages struggles with the rest of life. It may be
joyfully anticipated with the hope of what is to come or fearfully
dreaded with the despair over what has been left behind. As indicated by psycho-social theory, we can acknowledge the midlife
crisis, retirement, and losses of spouse, property and health, and so
on, by trying to comfort those feeling the pain of the struggle or we
can challenge them to lift their chin, keep going, and use and enjoy
what they still have. Or, we can perhaps minister in both senses at
once in continued growth toward spiritual well-being by offering an
alternative theological understanding of rest and striving with them
in their spirituality for new meaning within their unique experience
of human aging. Of course, new meanings are not limited to biblical
insight but with opened vision they do lend themselves to other circumstances, as in this instance with the saying "Today is the first
day of the *rest* of your life!" The ministry then, beyond the visit or
the teaching or the sermon or the counseling, is the spiritual instruction and inspiration that gives "the Way, the Truth and the Life,"
and enhances both the giver and the recipient toward a genuine
experience of God's peace.

SUMMARY AND NEW DIRECTIONS

Solid theological basis and careful spiritual focus lead to sound
ministry. It is not programs that succeed or fail, but ministry that is
done through them. Studied topics of individual expressions and ordered experience within the realms of religiosity and religion may
be useful for the church in assessing the relationship of the church in
aging, but they should not be determinative for the church's role. It

is from the vision and power of the church's own resources that the church should draw its theological imagery, set its spiritual goals, and evaluate its ministry's effectiveness. Those will lead us to the content of the church's role while the context is the complex process of human aging, or more particularly, the needs, problems and opportunities within the lives of aging persons.

Even though a developmental view of the aging process is more conducive to the sense of human striving and growth toward personal and social wholeness, the church needs to be assertive at that point as well in order to utilize its own theological themes of spiritual growth toward full maturity in Christ as a way of bringing new imagery and perspective to the meaning of life and experience of aging. Growing in faith, envisioning life through faith and maturing in our relationships with our God, with ourselves, with other persons, and with our world, suggest an alternative view of aging which we might term *spiritual aging*. Spiritual aging offers a new concept for identifying the perspective of the church's functioning relative to people throughout the aging process as it cuts across activity, disengagement and developmental theory to ask different kinds of questions and provide different kinds of responses. The development of spiritual aging as a concept and as a concern becomes the challenge now facing the church as it renews its commitment of service with and to the aging.

The discovery, then, is a role of the church in the field of aging which is not constrained by age, but is freed to relate to the aging of all ages. Such a role of the church is perhaps best assessed by the spiritually aging Christian laywoman, Maggie Kuhn, to be "the church's *continuing* role with the aging" (Hessel, 1977, emphasis added), namely to educate and nurture, to counsel, to serve as an extended caring family, to preach the Gospel, to provide social witness, and to deal with any special circumstances of aging issues, the aging process, and aging persons. To that degree, we may avoid an ageism of our own while taking seriously spiritual-religious concerns of people throughout the life span, and in so doing, embrace the challenge of how to proclaim the love of God in word and in deed in all the various social issues, personal concerns, and life changes associated with aging.

REFERENCES

Brown, J. Paul (1964). *Counseling with senior citizens.* Successful Pastoral Counseling Series (Russell L. Dicks, Gen. Ed.). Englewood Cliffs, NJ: Prentice-Hall.
Clements, William M. (Ed.) (1981) *Ministry with the aging.* San Francisco: Harper & Row.

Clingan, Donald F. (1975). *Aging persons in the community of faith. A guidebook for churches and synagogues on ministry to, for, and with the aging.* Indianapolis: The Institute on Religion and Aging and The Indiana Commission on the Aging and Aged.

Executive summary of Technical Committee on creating an age integrated society: Implications for spiritual well-being. (1981). The 1981 White House Conference on Aging, Department of Health and Human Services, Washington, DC: Author.

Fecher, Vincent J. (1982). *Religion and aging: An annotated bibliography.* San Antonio, TX: Trinity University Press.

Final report: The 1981 White House Conference on Aging. (1982). (Three Volumes). U.S. Department of Health, Education and Welfare, Department of Health and Human Services, Washington, DC: U.S. Government Printing Office.

Frankl, Viktor E. (1959). *Man's search for meaning: An introduction to logotherapy.* Boston: Beacon Press.

Frankl, Viktor E. (1971). *The will to meaning: Foundations and applications of logotherapy.* New York: New American Library.

Generations: Religion and aging (1983). *Generations, 8 (4),* entire issue.

Gray, Robert M. & Moberg, David O. (1962). *The church and the older person.* Grand Rapids: Eerdmans.

Hessel, Dieter T. (1977). *Maggie Kuhn on aging: A dialogue edited by Dieter Hessel.* Philadelphia: Westminster Press.

Hiltner, Seward (Ed.) (1975). *Toward a theology of aging: A special issue of Pastoral Psychology.* New York: Human Sciences Press. [Pastoral Psychology, *24* (229), Winter, 1975.]

LeFevre, Carol & LeFevre, Perry (Eds.). (1981). *Aging and the human spirit: A reader in religion and gerontology.* Chicago: Exploration Press.

Maves, Paul B. (1981). *Older volunteers in church and community: A manual for ministry.* Valley Forge, PA: Judson Press.

McClellan, Robert W. (1977). *Claiming a frontier: Ministry and older people.* Los Angeles: The University of Southern California Press.

Moberg, David O. (1968). Religiosity in old age. In Bernice L. Neugarten (Ed.), *Middle age and aging.* Chicago: University of Chicago Press.

Moberg, David O. (1971). *Spiritual well-being: Background and issues.* White House Conference on Aging, Washington, DC: U.S. Government Printing Office.

Moberg, David O. (Ed.) (1979). *Spiritual well-being: Sociological perspectives.* Washington, DC: University Press of America.

Nouwen, Henri J.M. & Gaffney, Walter J. (1974). *Aging.* Garden City, NY: Doubleday and Company. [Image Books edition, 1976.]

Reichert, Sara & Reichert, Richard. (1976). *In wisdom and the spirit: A religious education program for those over sixty-five.* New York: Paulist Press.

Sessoms, Robert L. (1977). *150 ideas for activities with senior adults.* Nashville: Broadman Press.

Thorson, James A. & Cook, Thomas C., Jr. (Eds.) (1980). *Spiritual well-being of the elderly.* National Intra-Decade Conference on Spiritual Well-Being of the Elderly, Atlanta, GA, 1977. Springfield, IL: Charles C. Thomas, Publisher.

Tilberg, Cedric W. (1984). *Revolution underway: An aging church in an aging society.* Philadelphia: Fortress Press.

Tournier, Paul. (1957). *The meaning of persons.* New York: Harper & Row.

Tournier, Paul. (1972). *Learn to grow old.* New York: Harper & Row.

Weiner, Marcella Bakur, Brok, Albert J., & Snadowsky, Alvin M. (1978). *Working with the aged: Practical approaches in the institution and community.* Englewood Cliffs, NJ: Prentice-Hall.

Issues in Publicly Subsidized Long Term Care Systems and Implications for the Religious Sector

John N. Morris, Ph.D.

ABSTRACT. Given the increasing numbers of elderly in need of long term care services and the harsh reality of finite resources, new models are required which define those elderly persons who should remain eligible for publicly subsidized long term care. If, in fact, a method is established for serving only a limited number of older persons, i.e., the truly vulnerable elderly, by way of the public system of long term care, a large constituency of older Americans will be left to exist on the margins. The church as an informal care system may appropriately assume the role of ensuring that the available public funds are used wisely and that service gaps inevitably left between the increasing number of older persons and shrinking public support are bridged. In addition, the church must assist in improving all long term care services by contributing to public policy formation.

Survival of the fittest is the law of the jungle. Fortunately, however, it is not the rule in the civilized world. In our society, compassion and a regard for human dignity dictate that the vulnerable elderly cannot be abandoned nor their needs ignored. In a world of infinite resources this commitment would be sufficient to protect those in need; but we do not live in such a world. I am not, however, unduly pessimistic about the possibilities for meaningful change. Most older people in need of care are receiving that help from family, friends and neighbors. For the most part, the formal system is used only to fill in gaps. Nevertheless, the current system does hurt some elderly people, and I believe more will be hurt unless some

John N. Morris is Associate Director, Department of Social Gerontological Research, Hebrew Rehabilitation Center for Aged, 1200 Centre Street, Roslindale, Massachusetts 02131.

151

changes are made. The reality is that prudence and an awareness of the limitations of both our resources and the willingness of the public to expend these resources for social programs makes it imperative that we develop new models to consider who should be excluded from publically subsidized care and who should remain eligible. It is likely that some people now receiving services will be excluded from services in the future because new definitions of need will be developed.

New definitions should be developed with local input. Community involvement will be of great value in deciding important questions such as who is to be served, how services are to be provided, what constitutes good quality of care, who will pay for this care and the level of quality of life outcomes we expect for the public dollars we spend.

Change is the only constant, and we can be certain that regulations and arbitrary rules are susceptible to change, especially if they are perceived as inappropriate or ineffective. It is generally agreed, for example, that the current Intermediate Care Facility (ICF) and Skilled Nursing Facility (SNF) definitions are not successful, and so it is likely that these regulations will be changed.

Moreover, the way long term care is financed is also subject to change. We need, and are seeing, an increase of private sector involvement in this area, for example, insurance efforts and the development of continuum of care retirement communities.

The question then becomes whether we are sliding rapidly downhill, going around in circles, or actually making some progress in our efforts to improve the long term care system. I believe we are making progress. We have learned a great deal in the past twenty years and we are better able both to describe the problems and to understand some of the causes of those problems. We do not need to re-invent the wheel; rather, we need to "tinker" with the system in order to improve its effectiveness.

DEFINING THOSE IN NEED OF LONG TERM CARE

One way to begin is to attempt to define precisely whom we mean by the vulnerable elderly. We must consider carefully how we identify the truly needy population, because without accomplishing this task successfully, we will be unable to meet the challenge of restructuring society's approach to the delivery of high quality long term care services.

First, there is that small proportion of the elderly suffering from catastrophic illnesses such as terminal cancer. Such people consume a large amount of our health/social service funds. The hospice program is one example of the cost beneficial ways that must, and I think will, be found to meet the needs of such people.

It is a person's ability to perform the functional activities that are a normal part of community living that is central to most long term care issues and problems. The designation of someone as at-risk or vulnerable generally carries with it the minimum requirement that the person is unable, either mentally or physically, to carry out independently one or more of the basic activities of daily living.

Historically four sets of factors have been considered in making such an assessment: self-care activities such as dressing and bathing; instrumental activities such as cleaning house and cooking; mobility, for example, climbing stairs or crossing a room; and medical conditions such as heart and neurological problems. It might seem at first glance that this last category would be the most helpful in assessing an elderly person's level of vulnerability, but such has not generally proven to be the case. Although there are linkages between a number of medical chronic conditions and reduced stamina, in most cases the correlation between disease states and functional impairment is not great. On a national basis, approximately 80 percent of individuals over 65 report the presence of one or more chronic conditions; yet only a small proportion of the elderly have reduced functional capabilities with normal activities of daily living.[1] It is functional status, therefore, rather than disease that dictates the vulnerability of this group.[2]

Once we have established a working definition of the vulnerable elderly, we should next determine how large a group we are talking about. Estimates are that of the 26 million Americans over 65 in 1981, about twenty percent or 5.2 million are functionally impaired.[1,3] About 14 percent, some 3.6 million, are thought to have problems with the activities of daily living severe enough to necessitate long term supportive services.[4] At least 80 percent of the elderly, therefore, are not restricted in basic areas of functioning, and do not require regular support services. It is only with the most elderly—those 85 and over—that general disability becomes the rule. It should be noted, however, that while 1 in 16 Americans is over 85 today, by the year 2035, it will be 1 in 10.[5] Therefore, there is reason to suppose that in the future both the number and the proportion of vulnerable elderly will increase.

What are the needs of these vulnerable elderly? The vast majority of those who are functionally vulnerable receive services from others, usually from family and friends.[6] In many cases, there is no need for any formal intervention because the elderly person's loved ones determine what care is needed and provide it. Without these services, vulnerable elderly persons would be unable to complete a variety of personal and instrumental activities of daily living. Some would be unable to bathe; others could not shop for food, while still others would seldom enjoy a hot meal. But while informal and formal services provide most elderly persons with someone they can depend upon for help, there are those with unmet needs, either because they have no outside supports, or more frequently because their needs have become too great and their informal supporters can no longer cope.

When a person has such an unmet need, a decision must be reached about whether formal agency service should be offered to compensate for the individual's functional deficiency. These judgments are complicated by the fact that the appropriate allocation of resources is becoming an issue of increasing importance. The decision on what is an appropriate level of service may depend on professional, regional, ethnic or political factors. A state such as Massachusetts, for example, has traditionally provided formal community supports at a higher level than most other states. However, in Massachusetts, as in most areas of the country, it is increasingly the case that key decision-makers define their service goals in terms of serving those elderly who are "most in need." That is to say those individuals who, without additional outside supports, would be in grave danger of institutionalization. In attempts to reach this targeted population, some programs have concentrated on outreach efforts, focusing on those living in poor or deteriorating neighborhoods or those about to be discharged from an acute hospital.[7] Others have looked at individuals who have actually applied for institutional placement or at those who are in institutions but might be capable of living in the community if additional service supports were provided at a reasonable cost.[8] In each of these situations, there is a need to determine who is and who is not appropriate for inclusion in the community service delivery system. Our present success in identifying those at risk of institutional placement has been limited, and we need to be in a position to better identify such persons.

In a study assessing the role of the Massachusetts Department of Elder Affairs in serving the vulnerable elderly, we presented crucial estimates of the proportion of people in the community requiring one or more formal home care service, as well as the proportion requiring a series of specific home care services.[9,10] In general, these estimates included those vulnerable elderly who were already receiving services, as well as those vulnerable individuals with an unmet need for additional care. It should be noted, that in some instances there were individuals with unmet needs who indicated that their informal support systems were prepared to meet all of these needs; they were included in the informal rather than formal service estimates. Seven service areas were examined, and we found that 17.2 percent of the elderly population required informal and/or formal support resources, with 17 percent (or 99 percent of those in need) already receiving at least some support services. Seen within the broadest categories, 10.5 percent receive all the needed supports, 6.5 percent receive some of the needed supports, and only two-tenths of one percent were receiving no support at all. Thus, 99 percent of the functionally vulnerable people in Massachusetts were receiving at least some of the care they required.

As I have already mentioned, family and friends are actively involved in the care of their loved ones. Slightly over half (51%) of the 17.2 percent of the elderly who require support services receive all of their needed care from family and friends. In most areas, relatives and friends provide the vast majority of the care received by the functionally impaired elderly in the community. In Massachusetts, for example, if one were to total up all of the hours of light housework support provided during any seven day period, 77 percent would come from informal sources. For meals, the informal provide 87 percent of the total supports, for shopping the estimate is 90 percent and, even for personal care, 74 percent of all support hours come from family and friends.

In our study of the Massachusetts Home Care Corporations, we also looked at the people who needed additional service supports and examined in what areas such supports were most needed. As might be expected, those who were actively seeking formal services were much more likely to be unable to cope with activities of daily living than the general aged population. For example, 14.2 percent of those in the general elderly population need assistance with light housework. Among those who applied for the Massachusetts Home Care services, however, 63.4 percent need such aid. Only 9.6 percent of the elderly in general need help in meal preparation, but 42 percent of the Home Care applicants are unable to prepare meals without help. The same pattern also exists for other activities. For example, 11.6 percent of older Americans cannot walk up and down stairs without assistance; among the Home Care applicants, more than half—52.5 percent—are unable to manage stairs independently. While only 5.5 percent of the larger population need help with personal care and 2.6 percent need help with medications, the proportion climbs to 23 percent and 13.2 percent respectively for Home Care applicants.

Based on the definitions of unmet need in the study, we found that the total proportion of vulnerable elderly in need of formal support services, equaled 8.5 percent of the elderly population as the proportion to be provided through the Massachusetts Home Care Corporations varied between 4.1 and 6.7 percent of persons 60 years of age or older in the community. The variation in the percentages depends on whether the Department of Elder Affairs (DEA) program services are targetted to those with severe unmet needs. The remaining persons among the 8.5 percent of the elderly population who require formal services, or about one quarter of the total requiring such services, receive all of their needed care from other formal agencies such as Medicare, Medicaid, etc.

DELIVERING THE SERVICES

Once the frail and dependent elderly have been identified, the question arises: how can these people best be served? Clearly, each such person is an individual with specific strengths and specific disabilities, and no single living arrangement or package of services will be right for all. There is a need for a whole range of long term care services including housing, meals, medical services and personal care, and it is important to match an individual's need with an appropriate environmental setting and level of service support, and then to check and make appropriate adjustments over time. This emphasis on the proper targeting of services is essential not only because of the issue of fair distribution of services in a time of scarce resources and rising costs, but also because better fit between the elderly person's needs and the level of service he or she receives is likely to result in a better quality of life.

At the present time, there is no coordinated continuum of care to ensure such fit. Rather, there is a patchwork of programs including institutions, adult day care, domiciliary care, sheltered congregate housing and home care. Consequently, the fit between people and programs is inexact at best, with some elderly people underserved and others receiving services for which they really have little need. The Massachusetts Home Care Service Corporations, mentioned earlier, represents a variant of the case management approach to improving the match between unmet need and the provision of services. While 20 percent of those in the general elderly population are functionally vulnerable, the proportion of the functionally vulnerable among those served by the Home Care corporation is between 85 and 90 percent. Indications are, therefore, that this case-managed program reaches those with functional deficits. At intake, as many as half of its clients can be defined as those with more severe unmet needs and almost all have some unmet needs. In the general population of functionally impaired elderly, however, over 90 percent have all of their needs met, and less than 5 percent have moderate to severe unmet needs. However, the high proportion of elderly in the community who receive all the care they need, cannot mask the problem that exists. Those seeking formal services tend to have heavy unmet needs in areas such as housework, personal care, and meals. The intake clients to Home Care had only 20 percent to two-thirds of their needs met, far short of the 90 percent level found for the general population of vulnerable elderly. However, following their entry into the program, the level of unmet need among these frail elderly people declined dramatically and began to approach the levels in the older group as a whole. A comprehensive program like this one can reduce levels of unmet need in most areas, although there are a few, such as transportation, on which the program seems to have little or no impact.

The Home Care Services Corporation also illustrates how a slight variation in the interpretation of just who is supposed to be caught in the government's "safety net" can drastically alter the proportion of individuals who will be cared for with public funds. If we only look at people with severe unmet needs, in a state like Massachusetts one could assume that the formal system is reaching 88 percent of all those who have real need. If, however, we look at all those who require some intervention beyond the informal, those with moderate or with a multiplicity of needs, as well as those with severe need, then the system appears to only be handling about 54 percent with 46 percent needing increased services. To put this difference in concrete terms, the difference in definition would add between 25 and 30 million dollars to the amount spent by Massachusetts yearly on long term care, and would add 12,000 elderly to those served. This variation accounts for the range of 4.1-6.7 in proportion of elderly estimated to be in need of Home Care Services.

It is certainly agreeable to look at a successful program, and much can be learned from the Massachusetts experience. Nevertheless, the problem of targeting services appropriately has not been solved. The use of institutions is one key issue that illustrates some of the problems in targeting long term care services appropriately. Few would argue that nursing homes do not have a place in long term care. They have been, and are likely to continue to be, the best, and perhaps the only alternative for those who need high-intensity 24-hour care. However, there is also a considerable amount of evidence that suggests that there are a number of people who are institutionalized who could remain in the community with the proper service supports. It has been found, for example, that persons without close relatives are more likely to enter long term care facilities with lower levels of need than those who have relatives.[11] These ''borderline'' individuals with moderate impairment, but with few informal supports, may choose a nursing home, not because it is truly their best alternative, but rather because other alternatives are either unavailable or unknown to them even if they have the economic resources to privately pay for alternative modes of care. In other cases, institutional placement is sought at the point of ''family burnout'' when informal supporters who have provided many services have reached a point at which they no longer feel they can provide adequate care.[12] Again, a nursing home is often chosen because it is perceived as the only alternative.

A good illustration of how many elderly people could be served in the community rather than in the more costly and restrictive nursing home is given in studies of the ACCESS Program in Rochester, New York.[13] ACCESS provided home care services to clients, almost all of whom were institutional applicants. Earlier in the program's history, we reported about 80 percent of the frail elderly were still in the community. Some nine months following community placement, these individuals had been successfully deflected from their earlier institutional path.

There is a difficulty, however, found by ACCESS and by other similar programs. The decision to enter a nursing home is not an easy one either for an individual or for a family. Once having made this choice, people are reluctant to consider other options.[14] The family is likely to resist referral to a community program after they have made up their minds that their elderly relative should enter a nursing home; outreach interventions that come after this decision come too late for most elderly; and binding pre-admission screening programs with access to needed community service alternatives are infrequent. Third party reimbursement, too, is geared toward the institutional rather than the home care alternatives.

It is also true that, while people who are severely impaired tend not to select themselves for programs providing too little care, and those on the borderline are unlikely to show up as applicants to alternative programs and more likely to apply for nursing home placement, light care individuals show up as applicants to almost all programs.[14] The implications of this situation are that when there are quotas, even with an outreach program, the program is more likely to serve the light care individuals who show up at the door first at the expense of those with greater need who may arrive later or who may be less likely to apply. For example, the functionally impaired constitute only 25 percent of the tenants of the average congregate housing project, not far different from the percentage of impaired elderly in ordinary housing.[15] The problem is that most such projects operate on a fixed budget and after initial rent-up, they have only about an 8 percent vacancy rate a year. They cannot meet their obligations unless they keep the apartments rented, and there is no inclination either to delay rent-up nor to specifically target these apartments for those with more severe need. Nor, are there any general models for reassessing the tenant populations to better determine who is being served.

By the same token, when pressures are weak on the system, a program that supposedly has rigid eligibility and service requirements can "bend" to the needs of the elderly population that is seeking services.

Obviously, the problems of delivering formal services appropriately are complex, but let us suppose for a moment that a solution to these problems is possible, and that only the most needy and the most vulnerable elderly will be served. This system would certainly be preferable for the extremely frail and dependent, and it would seem to be a fairer allocation of our finite resources. It is not that simple, however. Such a reform would leave a large number of elderly people living lives which, while supportable, would hardly be comfortable or agreeable. A large constituency of older Americans would be cut off from publicly supported services or placed on waiting lists. Those in this situation would exist on the margin, neither impaired enough for help nor independent enough to live well on their own. How are these people to be cared for?

THE ROLE OF THE CHURCH

The Church definitely has a role to play in assisting these people, as well as in the whole process of improving long term care. If lower care people are no longer helped by formal service programs, it is possible that they can be cared for by church programs such as day care centers, lunch programs and friendly visitors. Such programs are particularly valuable because they use many volunteers who are willing and eager to show fellowship to others without placing a burden on public resources. It may be that large numbers of people will call upon the resources of the church once they have been cut off the rolls of the formal service agencies. Yet, although the demand may seem overwhelming at first, it is important to remember that many people come for help when they are in a crisis situation such as a sudden illness or the death of a spouse. At the point of crisis, they need a number of hours of help, but that intense need is temporary. What we have found in looking at a number of programs is that for lighter and heavier care people, for those in congregate housing and those who live alone, in fact, for all but the most extremely isolated and impaired, the help that is needed is only *one hour a day*.[16] One hour a day can make the difference.

The Christian concept of social responsibility includes the involvement of the Church and its resources in efforts to improve community welfare. In the nineteenth century, when many churches had removed themselves from the social arena, a commentator wrote: "religion has withdrawn into isolated strongholds where it remains on the defensive, surveying the land through narrow loopholes in its fortifications." Fortunately, in the modern era, churches have been less likely to retreat and much more willing to enter into the fray in such areas as civil rights, war and peace and economic justice. Therefore, it is appropriate that the Church takes public positions and works to help clarify the goals of long term care.

Church organizations should help to develop and lobby for legislation that could be useful in this area. For example, the church might support legislation to permit the elderly to innovatively make use of the equity in their homes, or state income tax incentive programs designed to provide tax benefits to those who care for aged relatives, or tax incentives that would be of benefit to those who are willing to care for elderly non-relatives in their homes—in so-called domiciliary care programs.

Moreover, organizations like the Church are often in a better position to make caring decisions for people than is an impersonal bureaucracy. If churches, synagogues and fraternal organizations were included in a locally-based decision making process for allocating publicly available long-term care dollars, they would be more likely to be able to allocate those funds effectively and equitably than is now the case. The knowledge and the concern for people that goes into making a successful community of faith is the same knowledge and caring that could be used to provide appropriate and compassionate assistance to those in their last decades of life. Religious organizations could work toward developing and expanding fiscally responsible community-based services for the debilitated elderly, especially for those living alone in the community.

Another important public policy area in which the church could be involved is the creation of increased housing resources, including both congregate housing and domiciliary care. The use of such housing, in which support resources are built in at a minimal cost, may be preferable to either increased formal care or institutionalization. At the present time, however, it is difficult for a community service agency to secure reimbursement for such housing, and there are those in positions of power who resist the idea of building more supportive housing because of the construction and rent subsidy costs. The church could sponsor such housing and work to convince policy makers that trying to save money by not building supportive housing is a false economy since the type of person who requires this type of housing is likely to be the relatively low care individual who nursing homes often prefer, and nursing home residency is a far more costly option than supportive housing.

In addition to public policy formulation, the Church has an important role as a provider of long term care services. The Lutheran Church, of course, has a long and distinguished history of providing such services. It is important that the Church continue to run and to fund nursing homes, congregate housing, domiciliary care, and retirement housing for the impaired elderly. The Church hierarchy should identify where the gaps in care are, where actions could be taken quickly and where long term financial campaigns are needed. To the extent that religious organizations have models for administratively establishing high quality care facilities and high quality services in the community, procedures should be established for describing the types of processes, the arrangements with public funding sources such as HUD and Medicaid that appear to work, emphasizing particularly any procedures or administrative expertise that appear to make public regulatory agencies more confident and less restrictive in their dealings with service institutions.

The long term care alternatives that are created and run by the Church should be, in the words of Matthew, like "a city that is set on a hill," a model and an example of how such organizations should be run to provide the best and the most humane care possible.

Finally, the Church can be a source of advice and referral, and can disseminate information that helps channel people appropriately. Many older people who are ill at ease with the formal system and do not know where to turn can be reached through their local church, and families also can turn to the church to learn what alternatives are available to help their aged relatives. In this way, lonely and difficult decisions that seem irrevocable once they are made, can be replaced by informed choices made with community support.

Today, with the number of elderly people in our society steadily increasing, is not a time for the Church to retreat behind its fortifications. Rather, it is a time when the Church can and should play a pivotal role both in seeing that public funds are used wisely and appropriately and in bridging the gaps that will be inevitably left between growing numbers of old people and shrinking public support.

REFERENCES

1. *Health, United States: 1978* [DHEW Publ. No. (PHS) 78-1232], Washington, DC: U.S. Government Printing Office, 1978.

2. Campion, E.W., *Age Trends in Health Status.* Paper prepared as part of materials for Section 3.2, Health and Health Care Systems, background for 1981 White House Conference on Aging.

3. Nagi, S.Z., "An Epidemiology of Disability Among Adults in the United States," *Milbank Memorial Fund Quarterly,* 54(4): Fall, 1976.

4. Sherwood, S., J.N. Morris, C. Gutkin, et al., "The Needs of Elderly Community Residents of Massachusetts" (mimeo), Boston: Department of Social Gerontological Research, Hebrew Rehabilitation Center for Aged, 1977, p. 103. Final contract report, supported by research contract with the Survey Research Program, University of Massachusetts in connection with AoA Grant No. 90—A-641/01.

5. Administration on Aging, National Clearinghouse on Aging, *Some Prospects for the Future Elderly Population* [DHEW Publ. No. (DHDS) 78-20288], Washington, DC: U.S. Government Printing Office, January, 1978, pp. 125-178.

6. Morris, J.N. and S. Sherwood, "Informal Support Resources for Vulnerable Elderly Persons: Can They Be Counted On, Why Do They Work?" *International Journal of Aging and Human Development,* 18(2): 1983/84.

7. Eggert, G.M. and B.S. Brodows, "The ACCESS Process: Assuring Quality in Long Term Care," *QRB/Quality Review Bulletin,* February, 1982.

8. Morris, J.N. and C. Granger, "Assessing and Meeting the Needs of the Long Term Care Person," in *Adult Day Care: A Practical Guide,* C. O'Brien, ed., Belmont, CA: Wadsworth Publishing Co., 1983, pp. 125-126.

9. Department of Elder Affairs, Commonwealth of Massachusetts, "Needs Assessment Study for the Commonwealth of Massachusetts, 1982" Boston: Author, 1982.

10. Morris, J.N., S. Morris, and S. Sherwood, "Assessment of Informal and Formal Support Systems in High Risk Elderly Populations," in *Functional Assessment in Rehabilitation Medicine,* C. Granger and G.E. Gresham, eds., Baltimore: Williams & Wilkins, 1984.

11. Barney, J., "The Prerogative of Choice in Long Term Care," *Gerontologist,* 19: 309-314, 1977.

12. Podgorski, C.A. and T.F. Williams, "Predictors of Successful Home Care Plans." Report on research supported by AoA Grant No. 0090-AR-0036, June 1983.

13. Eggert, G.M. and B.S. Brodows, "Five Years of ACCESS: What Have We Learned?" *Home Health Care Services Quarterly,* 3/4: 17-48, 1984.

14. Sherwood, S., J.N. Morris, and Associates, "Alternative Paths to Long Term Care." A final report in connection with AoA Grant No. 90-A-1666.

15. Sherwood, S., J. Alfaro, U.K. Creditor, C.E. Gutkin, M. Holmes, E. Michelson, G. Miranda, and L. Schlesinger, "Performance Report I: The CHSP Participants." A report in connection with HUD Contract No. HC 5373, Evaluation of the Congregate Housing Services Program.

16. Morris, J.N. and G.M. Eggert, "One Hour a Day: Keeping the Functionally Vulnerable in the Community," *American Journal of Public Health,* submitted for publication.

Epilogue:
Exploring the Multiple Dimensions
of Aging

Joseph A. Sittler, B.D., D.D., Litt.D.

You have given me two tasks to do at the conclusion of this conference. First, I was to listen as carefully as I could to what I heard going on within one or another workshop, to read the preparatory literature, and to make what comments I wanted about the methodology by which you approached the discussion of your area of concern. Second, having done that, I was invited to add the kind of reflections upon aging which have occupied my attention for some years.

To the first job then. I think I articulated last night in a workshop with one of the groups my main concern about the methodology which characterized the church's inquiry into all areas of human concern. The term research probably came into prominence during the nineteenth century when historical study by chronical, legend, and recorded remembrance was replaced in the German historical school by the "scientific" historical method. The method is, to dig up the evidence, to find the coins, to search the documents, to look into the records, and really try to recreate for one time the events of a past time. That effort, which arose particularly in the natural and physical sciences and in history, became the normative method of research. As a result of the renown and reputation of the activity called research as it is used in the positive, empirical, mostly natural and physical sciences, all of us who are called to inquire into the way things are tend automatically to take our model of viable research from those sciences.

The term "research" must not be narrowed to the kind of reconstruction, evocation, discovery of data, which is appropriate to the natural empirical sciences. If we do that we self-limit our own discussion and the nature of our inquiry much too narrowly to open up—

Joseph A. Sittler is Distinguished Professor in Residence, The Lutheran School of Theology at Chicago, 1358 East 58th Street, Chicago, Illinois 60637.

discover—unfold—the very kind of thing we want to find out about aging.

Let me put it another way. If we think we can learn what the church needs to know about the interior drama of human aging by looking purely at the demographical, actuarial, clinical, medical, sociological data, we are not only deluding ourselves, but we are masking that delusion by the exterior influence of this very impressive statistical stuff. Statistical disclosures representative of facts are very important. To make them as responsible and accurate as possible is a right thing for any inquiring group to do. But we err to think that we can crack the present problem of how shall the ancient message of the divine redemption be most accurately, exactly, and redemptively addressed to the drama of aging.

Secondly, what is the internal nature of the circumstance for which we use the word "aging," with all the shifting notions of old, very old, fourth-quarter old, etc? I shan't talk about this as a category because you know all about it already, about the kind of investigation that is necessary to specify ever more clearly what kinds of groups we are dealing with. I want to talk now about this second item, the internal dimensions of aging.

What do I mean by "internal dimensions?" Purely empirical research is tempted to be contemptuous of the kind of reflective research which is required by the facts of human aging. The nuances to which reflection upon human aging must reflect delicately and precisely have a qualitative complexity which are central if we are to take seriously the internal drama of getting old. This kind of research dares to listen carefully to the never directly available, but only confessionally inferred realities of the internal dimensions of aging. This is what we've got to find research models for, research models with an eerie exactitude shaped to the requirements of the subject. Let me try to illuminate that even further. If there is such a thing as an internal drama of aging, what are the data for which a model must be devised? I would suggest that can never be directly known, but must be intuited by sensitive listening.

I would suggest that the clearest signals to what is the interior life of aging are provided by the aging themselves. The most important drama is, the internal testimony, the articulated pathos of aging as it exists in literature produced by and recognized as authentic by the aging. This testimony need not be a simple catalogue of their comments. Literary artists have carefully listened and have written works which constitute a rich condensation of the mood and pathos of aging. If one were to create an anthology of the most profound, moving, comprehensive statements about what it means to be growing old, to be highly self-conscious about aging, one could have an enormous book with literature all the way from Homer, Sophocles, Euripides, Cicero, St. Augustine, Dante, Milton, Shakespeare (marvelously in King Lear), the great metaphysical poets, and a whole cartload of contemporary literary people. The literature produced by the aging about aging is the confessional corpus from which our understanding must be ripened and matured.

I want to illustrate that point with several statements and ask you to think about them because they are representative of a vast amount of literature. I know this task requires contemporary research experts to do something which most of them are not really prepared to do, and because of the prestige of models of research shaped in other disciplines, they are reluctant to undertake it. But I think we can overcome this reluctance and train ourselves to do it or give up this job as not proper to us. To listen to something that cannot be reduced mathematically to statistics is an unpopular enterprise.

There are some things that cannot be done that way, so I give you an illustration. I recall a short story. The author talks about two old people sitting in the sun on an October afternoon, in a southern place, looking out over the high hills that cup the valley in which this old couple live. The old man says to this wife, "Anna, not many days now until there will be snow on those peaks." The author asks us to weigh this. Anna knows as well as John that it's October; they both know that winter is coming. Why is something perfectly obvious made the subject of a sentence, "pretty soon now there will be snow on those peaks?" The author says, does not the banal, ordinary, run-of-the-mill statement from the old man say that the coming of the snow on the distant peaks is a kind of symbol of the interior drama of the periodicity of all life? We move from July to September to October. The vast, the implacable unfolding of time into an irreversible never-again-to-be recovered momentum of time.

This is a kind of silent signal of the pathos of aging. If we, in our too snappy assumption, think that we can uncover that in research methods not molded exactly to it, we are dead wrong. This is the interior thing. The church, more than any other community ought to be sensitive to this. The church has the knowledge, the wisdom, the revealed word of God to say that all life moves from life into death. The church ought to have both the courage and the concreteness to say that aging is not an ordinary problem. Ordinary problems look for solutions. To the problem of aging, there is no solution. We must not talk about all things as if they could be solved. The problem of aging is not solvable, it is only acceptable, tolerable, received in grace, forgiveness, and love.

That recalls to me my second illustration. I have probed over the years for a single term with which to specify the exact anatomy of this pathos. This quest operates within the larger mystery of time itself. It was St. Augustine who best pointed to this mystery. He said that each of us knows what time is and added, "But if you ask me to explain, I know not." We too know something of this mystery of it. Time is relentless forward-leaning movement. The past is rememberable but not reversible. If I have sought to find a term to express that, I have found several ways to not fully express it because fundamentally it is not expressable. Such a pointing is A. E. Houseman's little poem about the man in midlife returning to the country that he had first visited in youth.

> When first my way to fair I took,
> few pence in purse had I;
> And long I used to stand and look
> At things I could not buy.
> Now times are altered;
> if I choose to buy a thing, I can;
> For here's the purse and here's the fair,
> but where's the lost young man?

Aging without a sense of infinite and implacable diminishments is not possible. The interior drama of aging can only be expressed with any kind of comprehensiveness by the word "pathos." That does not mean that it is all without joy or hope, or certainly for the Christian believer, faith and love. But it is pathetic. We must not talk about the ultimate pathos as being sociologically solvable. It is not solvable. The language reportorial of that clear sense can be found in a Shakespearean sonnet. The four verses that open the fourteen line sonnet have as their context the knowledge that the year moves from spring through the blooming greenness of summer into the autumnal somber ones of October. The lines are as follows:

> That time of year thou mayest in me behold
> When yellow leaves or few or none to hang along
>   these boughs
> that shake against the cold,
> Bare ruined choirs where late the sweet bird sang.

Which one of us moving from young life through maturity, into old age, could hear that last line, "Bare ruined choirs where late the sweet bird sang," without a pang? These songs are followed by the faltering memory, the dimming of the clear outlines of the actual, the quiet departures of the death of our friends, the appalling changes in the faded youthful theaters of experience.

Now therefore, what I am calling upon you to inquire, to investigate, to make yourself sensitive to, is this: when the church, the community of grace and faith, talks about aging, deals with the interior drama of aging in a proclamatory, liturgical, devotional, comforting way—take the dimensions of what you are doing seriously.

One among many things that the church must refine her practice of is in the area of preaching on the meaning of eternal life. Now this is a whopping subject and I want to give you only the bare outline of what I am thinking. Death is not something that we ought to preach about only at funerals. Such a theme is too big to explore sensitively only when a death has signalized an event in a congregation. The preaching about life ought always include life leaning irreversibly towards death. So that one is prepared for death by life. One learns how to deal with death while living, not just on the edge of collapse. The great philosopher Martin Heiddeger says, "the moving into old age is at time of releasement 'Gelassenheit,' a time of letting loose, learning to let go, to consent to being, to let be." Now these are profound terms. The church of all intellectual and religious communities has, I think, the deepest store of lived experience upon which to learn how to deal with it.

Let me talk about preaching. I am an old beat-up preacher, and I spent a lot of my life doing it. What is the usual meaning that our people have, what meanings do they attach to the word that begot essays all the way from the *Reader's Digest* on up, called "Life after Death," Kübler Ross and all that? What do our people commonly understand about life after death? In the first place, most of them expect some form of it. Most of them have rather clear scenarios of what at best it must be. Most people mean by life after death a kind of selective and endless reenactment of the better moments of life before death. They want the best things, or the most enjoyable things, or the most enduring values that they have experienced in life to be replicated in some strange mystical way after death.

This has little to do with biblical teaching about life after death. In fact, I think we ought to drop the phrase in favor of an investigation, not only by theologians in the classroom, but by preachers in the pulpit, of the biblical language of eternal life. The phrase is an alluring one precisely because of its illogicality. What we mean by the word life is clear. It is that awareness of the period between coming into and passing out of existence. From the time of my birth to the time of my demise, this is life. Life in ordinary logic and experience can only mean that bracketed periodicity and duration in which I am, or my brothers and sisters in this mortal experience are, and have been. That is life. The term is temporal, mortal, characterized by passingness. How can we ever use the word "eternal" about something whose substantial interior meaning is temporal and passing? And yet the scriptures do use the word, "eternal life." I am shocked by the fact that I have seldom heard a sermon about the meaning the term has in Scripture. I never in my own parish heard my own pastor talk about the meaning of eternal life, and therefore, by not talking about it, or not unfolding the biblical use of the language, we permit people to carry on this partly secular and partly banal notion that eternal life means the same as some lovely country club after death. This is disobedient, bad biblical teaching and reprehensible preaching.

In the scripture, there is no effort at all to fill with historical specific content the word "eternal life." Paul made a couple of shots at it in Thessalonians and Corinthians when he was asked "in what body shall the dead arise?" He tried a couple of answers. Significantly, he never tried them twice. He talks about how there is one flesh of fowl, and one fish, and one of animals, and he gave it up as a bad job. And at the end of his discussions of these matters, in the letter to the Romans, he had this summary sentence, "If we live we are the Lord's, if we die we are the Lord's; therefore brethren, whether we live or whether we die, we are the Lord's." Or putting it into a concrete, core statement, "In death, as in life, we are the Lord's."

That is the biblical teaching. That as we come from God by his creativity, by his gift of the breath of life by which we are called into existence, so if we are in Christ, we are in him, and he does not die. Therefore, in death as in life we are the Lord's. Or to put it as Willie Marxsen puts it, "the Bible makes no effort to propose a scenario for the exact agenda of life after death."

We must disabuse our people of these strangely secular, materialistic and worse, utterly egocentric notions of eternal life, and teach them that the doctrine of eternal life means that if you are in Christ, and Christ in you, you now and forever participate in the deathless life of God.

This effort properly to reconceive the scripture-language about eternal life is going to take some doing. Most of our preaching and teaching and devotional life, certainly liturgical admonition, is an invitation to move life beyond its clamant egocentricity. The essential intention of Christian nurture is to displace the clamant ego by the gospel of God's kingdom. How strange, then, that our understanding of eternal life should curve the mind backward upon the egocentric concern with self-preservation. How is it then that when we talk about eternal life people say, "what's going to happen to me?" The Bible says that is not the most important question. The Christian faith says, "Eye hath not seen, nor ear heard, the things that God hath prepared for them that love him." Put another way, if all my life, my education, my culture, my only partly successful efforts to understand what it means to be and become a Christian, always are causing me to transcend my own identity, God knows I don't want to spend eternity replicating Joe Sittler forever and ever. I've got more ambition than that. So that this notion of eternal life as being an eternal enthronement of the ego in its most self-congratulatory and pleasant historical existence, is not only not Christian, it's positively blasphemous. Now we've got to get at that. If we are going to bring the gospel for the aging into a dimension that is big enough for the dreams, the hopes, the fears, the pathos of aging, it has got to be something more than the Sun City Antiseptic Community forever and ever.

In summary, let me say first that we should shape research models to the sobriety of the material. Let us try to fashion models that have the exquisite inwardness of the thing we are dealing with. And how do we learn about that? Read Tolstoy's *The Death of Ivan Illich.* It is worth a dozen reports on the clinical aspects of aging. Or read the great confessional literature of the aging, and the world's literature is full of it. So that we have to, as it were, find what we call input of another order. What we are up to here is not just a fresh goosing of the mind of the church towards a new kind of program, it is a new kind of inquiry we have got to undertake with fresh sensibilities.

I conclude with a wonderful statement from the last act of "King Lear." There is a kind of Christian equivalent to the beautiful passage in which Lear, having had his idolatrous mind cleared of his own egocentricity, having beheld the frivolity of the declared love of his two daughters, Regan and Goneril, and having had certified the genuine love of the right one, Cordelia, and as a broken, bereft, blind old man, he finally sees, and Shakespeare has the wonderful term, "Man must endure his going hither, even as his coming hence, ripeness is all."

You know the Christian phrase "if we live, we are the Lord's, and if we die, we are the Lord's." That is a kind of Christian statement in Christian terms, of ripeness is all. That is, old age for the reflective is a time of "coming to ripeness," with a kind of wry and godly sense of humor. Old age is beholding the truth about oneself, of the ambiguous actualities that underlie one's public reputation, if I may put it so. To become aware that we are all in a sense a marvelous mixture of good and evil, of eccentricity and public honor, and it is before God, it is only by grace. To understand that is an interior ripening. Man must endure his going hither even as his coming hence, ripeness and all.

Index

ACCESS program, 158-159
Administration on Aging, 14,33
Advocacy role, 61
affective loading, 35-36
ageism, 139
aging
  behavioral factors in, 42
  belief systems and, 37-38
  biological, 44-46,50-52
    retarded, 118-119
  concepts of
    contemporary, 33-35
    historical, 31-33
  demography of, 6-7,31-32
  as disease, 34
  environmental factors in, 34-36
  faith's role in, 140
  genetic factors in, 48,49
  "interior life" of, 166-172
  as intrinsic process, 46
  literary portrayal of, 42,166-167,
    168-169,171-172
  medical criteria for, 41-42,50-51
  metaphors of, 36-38
  multifactorial nature of, 33
  multiple dimensions of, 165-172
  pathos of, 166-169
  physiological function decline in, 45
  physiological integration in, 50-51
  pleiotropic nature of, 49
  research in, 165-166
  social implications of, 5-6,11
  spiritual, 149
  spiritual development and, 127-136
    Church's role in, 134-136
    identity and, 130-131
    memory and, 128-131
    prolepsis and, 127,131-132
    time concepts of, 132-133
  stereotypes of, 57
  terminology of, 138-139,143-146

theories of, 47-50,139-142
  homeodynamic, 50-51
  scientific, 139-142
Aldrich, Robert, 34
Alzheimer's disease, 92
American Experience of God, An
  (Farina), 130
arteriosclerosis, 32
Augustine, Saint, 168

baby boom, 6,122, *see also* aging,
  demography of
Ball, Robert, 70
behavioral factors, in aging, 42
belief systems, 37-38
Bible studies, 103
biography, religious, 134
biological age, 44-46,50-52
  retarded, 118-119
biological time, 45-46
Birren, James, 125
Buddhism, 124

Camus, Albert, 24
cancer, life expectancy and, 46,47
capital equity, of long-term care, 69-77
cardiovascular disease, life expectancy
  and, 46,47
career change, 119-120
Catholic Charities, 106
Christianity, spiritual development and,
  124
Church
  advocacy role of, 61
  capital assets of, 12
  elderly's attendance rates, 100
  as informal support system, 60-62
  leadership of, 13-14
  long-term care role of, 160-162
  membership of, 12